# How to Develop your Psychic Power

## Richard Webster

# How to Develop your Psychic Power

Written by Richard Webster

Illustrated by David Britland

Published by Martin Breese

First Published 1988


**Martin Breese Ltd: 164 Kensington Park Road,
Notting Hill Gate, London W11 2ER, England.**

ISBN 0 947533 08 7

*Other titles by the same author include:*

THE SECRETS OF GHOST WRITING
HOW TO READ MINDS
DISCOVERING NUMEROLOGY
HOW TO READ TEA LEAVES
THE STARS AND YOUR DESTINY
SUN SIGN SUCCESS
HELP YOUR CHILD WITH PALMISTRY
FREEDOM TO READ

# CONTENTS

# INTRODUCTION

You are psychic! Yes, you may not be aware of it yet, but you are psychic. I have conducted classes and lectures on psychic subjects for many years in several different countries, and I have yet to find someone who did not possess psychic abilities.

Think back over your life and recall the instances when you felt you just had to contact someone, and at that instant the phone went and it was the person you had been thinking about. Remember the times when you had a strong feeling that someone was not well, and when you checked up found that your feelings had been correct. Maybe you have had premonitions in your dreams, or suddenly felt that something was not right with a person you had just met. All of these are examples of your psychic abilities in action.

It is even possible for us to use our psychic abilities and not be aware of it. For instance, many years ago research was done on the numbers of people travelling on a train on the day it crashed. Investigators checked the numbers of people on the same train one day, one week, two weeks and three weeks before the day of the accident, as well as one week after. To their surprise, they discovered that there were always fewer people on the trains the day they were involved in accidents. Why was this? The people who would normally have been on the train could offer no explanation. Either they had slept in, felt ill, or couldn't be bothered going to work that morning. There was no consistent explanation, but something kept those people off their usual train on the day it crashed! To my mind, this represents unconscious ESP (extra-sensory-perception). The people were unaware of it, but something inside them prevented them from catching a disaster-bound train.

So, even if you are certain that you have the psychic awareness of the average oyster, you do have latent abilities, and the purpose of this book is to help you develop these abilities to the stage where you could become a professional psychic if you wished to.

Please do not skip chapters on the first reading. The book is deliberately set out in a step by step order to help you develop your skills. It might be a good idea to read through the book quickly, before returning to the start. Go through each chapter properly, but do not miss anything out. Each chapter is of equal importance.

Good luck.

CHAPTER ONE

# THE WORLD OF ESP

ESP (or extra-sensory-perception) is simply another way to describe your intuition or sixth sense. It is an extra sense that we all have, and there is nothing mysterious about it at all.

ESP is divided up into a number of areas - telepathy, clairvoyance, precognition (or premonition) and psychokinesis (usually called PK for short).

Telepathy is another name for mind reading, the ability to pick up someone's thoughts. Usually this is a two way process. One person concentrates on something and a second person tries to pick up what that thought may be.

Clairvoyance is the ability to know something without picking it up from someone else's thoughts. For instance, if you knew that under a certain rock you would find three snails and a grasshopper, you would be gaining that information clairvoyantly. Many psychic researchers class telepathy and clairvoyance as being the same thing, and of course, there will be many instances when you will pick up information, yet not know where the information came from, so it could well be either telepathy or clairvoyance. You may have heard of Psychometry. This is where someone picks up feelings and vibrations by holding on to something belonging to someone else, usually a ring or other personal belonging. Psychometry is an example of

Clairvoyance in action.

Precognition (or prediction) is the ability to foresee something that has not yet happened. This ability to see into the future is something we all expect if we go to a psychic reader.

Psychokinesis (or PK) is the ability to influence an object or event by using the power of our minds. Uri Geller's ability to bend spoons could well be an example of PK in action. A more useful example would be the ability to heal sick people by spiritual or psychic healing.

We will be discussing them all in greater depth later on. You will find that you are naturally better at some of these than others, but it is my hope that you will develop ability in all areas. You may have read of the many talents of the American psychic, Ingo Swann. He is especially good at PK and has been able to influence the breakdown rate of radioactive material simply using the power of his mind. Radioactive substances break down at a standard rate, so the ability to slow that rate down, or to speed it up, is a significant example of PK, and one that can be measured by scientists. So Ingo Swann is unusually gifted in this direction, but he is also talented in the other main areas of ESP.

Parapsychology is the name of the branch of science that studies ESP, and parapsychologists are the scientists involved in this field. Scientific interest in this area is comparatively new, and even today parapsychology laboratories find it hard to obtain enough funds to do all that they would like. You have probably heard of Dr J. B. Rhine of Duke University in the United States. His studies, and writings, dating from the 1930s were the first to bring popular attention to this field. Amongst other things, he

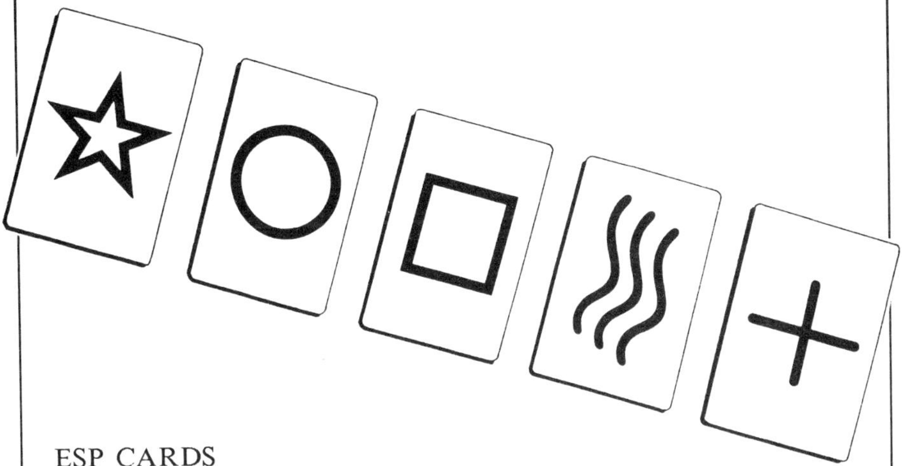

ESP CARDS

devised ESP cards which were used for many years to test people's ESP abilities. These cards consisted of five different designs, repeated five times each - a star, circle, square, three wavy lines and a plus sign. They were chosen because they were supposed to be easy to transmit and receive. The idea was that the pack was mixed and a number of experiments could be done with them. For instance, telepathy could be demonstrated by having someone look at the top card and send that thought to the person being tested. Clairvoyance could be tested by having the pack mixed and the person being tested would go through all the cards one at a time 'guessing' at what he thought each one was. Even precognition could be tested with these cards. The person being tested would write down the order he thought the cards would be in after they were mixed.

Dr Rhine also did many experiments with dice, and you can see gamblers trying to influence the throw of the dice in the same way today!

Gradually, the type of testing used by parapsychologists changed and became more and more sophisticated. If you were to be tested at a parapsychological laboratory today you would probably be asked to play a computer game. You may not even feel as if you were being tested at all!

In the Soviet Union, parapsychology is being taken extremely seriously. You can see why, when you stop to think of the consequences if someone behind the Iron Curtain were able to influence the mind of the President of the United States! A few years ago that might have made a good science fiction plot, but Russian parapsychologists believe that it is actually possible.

Well, enough of the theory for now. Let's get on to the next chapter and start some practical experiments.

## CHAPTER TWO

# RELAXATION

This may seem like a strange subject in a book on psychic development, but it is, in fact, possibly the most important chapter in the book. It is essential that you can relax at will to fully utilise your psychic potential.

"Of course, we can all relax," you might be thinking. True, but let's try a little experiment. Find yourself a comfortable chair which allows you to sit with your feet flat on the floor and provides good back support. Hold your left arm in front of your body about the level of your chest. Place the forefinger of your right hand into the palm of your left hand. Concentrate on relaxing all the muscles of your left arm and hand. Imagine all the muscles relaxing. Once you have done this, and feel that your left arm and hand is completely relaxed, count slowly to three. On the three, quickly remove your right forefinger.

Have you done that? If you were properly relaxed your left hand and arm would have dropped into your lap. If you were tense and not relaxed, your hand would have stayed in mid air. It's not as easy as we think.

Let's try a proper relaxation exercise. Sit back in your chair and make sure that you will not be disturbed for half an hour. If you are on your own take the phone off the hook whilst you try this exercise. Make sure the room is reasonably warm, too. As you have to do this exercise with your eyes closed, read through the next paragraph a few times before starting.

Sit back in your chair, with your hands in your lap and your feet flat on the floor. Start taking deep breaths, holding them for a few seconds before exhaling. As you exhale, say to yourself 'relax!' After about ten deep breaths close your eyes and concentrate on relaxing the muscles at the top of your head. Once you feel that you have achieved this imagine the relaxation flowing over into the rest of your body. Feel your face muscles relaxing, your neck muscles, your shoulder muscles. Imagine the relaxation slowly moving down one arm all the way to the tips of your fingers, and then going down the other arm. Feel your trunk muscles relaxing, the muscles of your stomach, then down one leg to the tips of your toes. Feel them tingle with relaxation. Then go down the other leg all the way to the tips of your toes. Take your time, making certain that each part is completely relaxed before moving on to another area.

Stay there awhile in this peaceful, relaxed state. Be aware of how relaxed you are; how all the strain and cares of the world have faded away. Imagine that you are floating effortlessly through space. Nothing bothers you. All is peaceful and calm.

After several minutes of this relaxation slowly come back to the real world, by counting from one up to ten. Once you reach ten, open your eyes and have a good stretch.

Do you feel better after that? You should do. The tensions of everyday life leave their mark on all of us, and it does your whole system good to take time out to completely relax. If you are tense you will not relax properly even when fast asleep. This is why you sometimes wake up in the morning feeling as if you have gained nothing from your night's rest. If you have trouble sleeping, simply go through this exercise once you go to bed and you will find yourself dropping off to sleep very easily.

Practice this exercise every day until you can completely relax in just a few seconds. With a little practice you will be able to do it just as easily with your eyes open. I can do it almost anywhere at any time and find it very useful. If I have to wait for traffic lights, I simply relax so that no tension builds up. If I have to wait to see someone I go through this exercise. Some days I may not do it at all, but on other days I may do it several times.

Now, what does this relaxation have to do with ESP? It simply makes it much easier for the psychic impulses to get through if you are completely relaxed. For several years I conducted what were known as 'Horoscope Parties' in people's homes. These were demonstrations of telepathy, clairvoyance and precognition, climaxed with some crystal ball gazing. I found that my most successful demonstrations occurred on evenings when I felt calm and relaxed about everything. If I had an argument with my wife before leaving home, all the demonstrations suffered. So I had to remain calm and relaxed to do my best work.

Most psychics believe that everyone and everything on this globe is interconnected, and I find this idea very useful in any ESP demonstration. I simply relax, imagine myself being in harmony with everything, and then think about whatever it is I am attempting. For instance, if I was wanting someone to contact me, but did not know how to locate them, I would go through the relaxation exercise, see myself as being in tune with the universe (including the person I was trying to locate) and then gently will that person to contact me. I think it would be possible to do it without relaxing first, but it would take longer and be much more difficult.

You may have related these relaxation exercises to hypnotism, as this is actually the first stage of self hypnosis. So, once you are completely relaxed you can programme your mind to do anything - from stopping smoking to gaining more confidence. We will not go into this here, but we will be doing exactly that to help you increase your psychic abilities.

Firstly, you will have to record a cassette which you will play every time you do the relaxation exercise. Here is a suggested transcript for you to use, but feel free to devise your own. You will notice that in this transcript I mention lazing around in a boat on a lake. That works very well for me as I enjoy being out in small boats, but it could well be the worst thing to say for you if you are scared of the water. If this is the case, simply devise a peaceful scene for yourself that is not worrying. For instance, you might see yourself lying down in a grassy meadow on a summer afternoon, or you might imagine yourself floating around on a fluffy white cloud - it can be anything, just as long as you find the scene relaxing. It can even be an actual place you know, as long as you have experienced nothing but happiness there. Here is my transcript:

Firstly a period of silence as I relax completely. If you wish you can include in your cassette your entire relaxation routine. I do not do that myself, but it may prove helpful to you. Now the message.

"It is so peaceful and quiet. I am so relaxed, so totally relaxed, just floating here feeling the gentle lapping of the water on the sides of my boat. It is so relaxing, so peaceful. The clear blue sky, the blue blue water, and I'm just floating, so calmly. So, so relaxed. In this nice, calm, peaceful relaxed state I am aware of every fibre of my being. I'm aware of every part of me being so relaxed. My brain is awake, ready to absorb and retain every idea put to it. My subconscious is awake, calmly waiting for suggestions. I can see myself becoming more intuitive, more psychic. My feelings are strong and getting stronger. If I have feelings about things in the future I will stop and pay attention to them. I am psychic, I am aware. Nothing can stop my subconscious from growing and steadily developing its intuition. I am psychic and becoming more intuitive with each passing day. In particular my abilities are growing in the area of (in here put the area you are working on at the time. For this example we will use psychometry.) psychometry. Whenever I wish it to happen, I will feel vibrations and pick up messages from items I hold. I will do so in a calm, relaxed manner, to help my subconscious come through with the right messages. Every time I do a psychometry reading my abilities will increase, both in psychometry and in all aspects of the psychic. I am a psychic, and every day my abilities grow. Whenever I need help or guidance I will relax and return to my beautiful boat floating in a blue, calm lake, and gaze at the clear blue sky and let my intuition take over. It is so peaceful and so relaxing. So peaceful and so relaxing. Now, on the count of ten I will slowly wake up and return, calm and relaxed, to my everyday world. 1, 2, 3, 4, gradually waking, 5, 6, 7, eyes opening slowly, 8, 9 and 10. I am wide awake."

When you make your own personal cassette, record the message slowly, allowing plenty of space between individual sentences. Don't be afraid to allow as much as half a minute go by without sound. In your relaxed state, time means nothing, so take as much time as possible in recording the message.

Put anything you like in the message, but make it all positive, as your mind will react more easily to those suggestions. For instance, "I will not smoke in the future" is not nearly as powerful a message to hear in the relaxed state as "I am a non-smoker".

Experiment with your cassette. No one need ever hear it except for you, so there is no need to be bashful. If a friend or relation makes you feel relaxed and comfortable, talk about them in your cassette. You will be changing your message as we work on each chapter. You may like to keep your cassettes, so that you can play one when you want to work on developing your telepathy and another one if you are working on your precognitive abilities.

You will find all of this much easier if you are able to set aside a regular time each day for the relaxation exercise. After doing this for a few days you will find yourself looking forward to your own special quiet time. You will notice other benefits in your life as well. You will be able to handle difficult situations much more easily. There will be less strain and tension in your life. Your confidence will improve. You will even start to look younger as the relaxation exercises will remove strain lines from your face. Oh yes, it will also increase your psychic awareness.

CHAPTER THREE

# TELEPATHY

Now that you can relax at will, we can start on developing your psychic abilities. If you can not relax whenever you wish to, stay on chapter two until you can.

Telepathy is simply another name for mind-to-mind communication. Think back over the times in your life when you have been in touch with the mind of another person. It may have been something trivial, such as you and a friend saying exactly the same thing at the same time - or it might have been extremely important, such as suddenly knowing that someone close to you was in danger. Try and recapture the feelings you had then. Don't hurry with this. Get yourself into a relaxed state and start to think about the experiences of this nature you have already had. You may be surprised at the number of telepathic experiences you have already had!

Once you can recapture exactly how you felt on previous occasions, when you were in telepathic communication with others, you are in a strong position to do it, whenever you wish to communicate mentally with someone else.

We will start with an experiment that you can do on your own. Make sure that you will not be disturbed for about half an hour and go to the place where you do your relaxation exercises. Relax completely, then think about someone you have not been in contact with for a while.

Visualise them as if they were in the room with you. Once you have them completely in your mind, let them go - simply relax again for a few minutes. Then visualise your friend doing whatever it is they are likely to be doing at this very moment. Don't force any impressions to come through. Let your mind float and absorb anything that comes into it. You may get a picture of your friend doing something mundane like washing the dinner dishes. They may be doing something you may not have expected, such as sitting in a picture theatre, or having a bath! If you get a strong impression such as this, check it out later, as you will be experiencing this clairvoyantly- which means that you are a chapter ahead!

No matter whether you picked up a distinct impression or not, you will have a clear picture of your friend in your mind. Hold that picture for as long as your can. When you feel your mind beginning to wander, bring it back by willing your friend to contact you. Firstly, re-experience the feelings you had when you were previously in telepathic communication with someone else. Then send your message. You may do it something like this:

"Bill, I'm thinking about you. I know that you will be picking my thoughts up. Please give me a ring, or contact me in some way. Please phone, Bill. I'm waiting for you to ring. Bill, you are getting a strong desire to contact me. Please come through, Bill. Come on, contact me now."

Keep this sort of message up for about five minutes. It doesn't matter if you keep on repeating yourself, just as long as you feel yourself sending the message to your friend. After five minutes, gradually waken yourself by counting slowly to ten. Try not to think about your friend at all now until the following morning.

If your friend was a particularly good subject, he may ring you even before you come out of relaxation. If he contacts you that same evening, congratulations! You have proved that you are good at transmitting telepathically. What if he doesn't ring? There could be a number of reasons for this. He may have picked up your thoughts but been unable to contact you for some reason. He may have had to take an unexpected trip and be thousands of miles away.

After doing this exercise, do anything else you wish, but try not to think about your friend. The following day give him a ring. Do not mention your attempts to make contact telepathically. You may be surprised to find that he mentions it first.

"I had a strong impulse to ring you last night," he might say. "I was going to, but thought it was a bit late. Fancy you ringing now!"

This is obviously a successful test, also. However, what do you do if he makes no mention of thinking about you? Simply try the experiment again with another person. It may take several attempts to have a successful contact, but each time you try it you are gaining experience, and each attempt will bring you closer to ultimate success.

Once you can do this test whenever you feel like it, try broadening the limits. Try and contact someone you do not know well and see what happens. For some reason it is always easier to contact people we feel strongly about, such as relations and friends. It is a great deal harder to contact someone you may only vaguely know at work. Yet, if the next morning they say they thought about you the previous evening, you will know that your abilities are increasing rapidly.

When I was at school I wasted a lot of time by staring at the back of the person in front of me, willing them to turn around. You may have tried this type of experiment yourself and been surprised at how it always works. I used to take it several steps further until I could get everyone in the class to turn and look in my direction! This is an example of telepathy in action, as my thoughts would gradually impinge on the other person until they had to look in my direction. You can try this sort of experiment anywhere. If you are on a long bus ride, concentrate on the person in front of you and will them to turn around. Try doing it in a picture theatre before the film starts, or anywhere else where people gather. This is an extremely useful test as all of these people will be strangers, making the test that much harder.

Once you can do this you can make the test even harder. Instead of having them turn around and look at you, you could make them look upwards, or perhaps scratch their nose. This is pretty advanced, though, so do not expect immediate success.

For most experiments in telepathy you will need a partner. Choose this person very carefully. It will need to be someone who is interested in what you are doing, someone who will encourage you, rather than say you are wasting your time. A good indication would be if the person has the same sense of humour as you. Do not choose someone simply because you happen to be married to them, or they live next door. Of course, those people might be ideal, but on the other hand, they may ridicule your efforts and undermine your confidence. If you found it particularly easy to contact someone in the first experiment, that person might make an ideal partner.

After you have found the right person, teach them how to

relax before trying any of these experiments.

This is a very simple test. Have your friend hold both hands out, palms up, in front of them. Ask them to close their eyes, relax and think of one of their hands. As soon as you feel an impression reach over and touch the hand you feel is the one being thought about. Do this five times, and then swap around so that you are holding out your hands and your friend is trying to pick up your thoughts. When you first try this, say "Yes" or "No" after each attempt. Once you get consistent results, do a run of five before announcing the result. The reason for this is that as a hit will feel different to a miss, you can learn from both your successes and failures.

This is a comparatively easy test, as the odds are only one in two, so you should get at least half right even if you are simply guessing. However, it is a start. Once you can get this test correct most of the time, try the next one. The odds are still only one in two, but it makes a change.

Take a deck of cards and mix them thoroughly. Have your partner look at the top card and concentrate on its colour - red or black. After you have made your choice and named a colour, he is to show it to you and then replace it somewhere in the middle of the deck. The reason for this is that it is possible to know if more red cards have appeared than black during a run, so you could increase your chances of success by calling out the colour that had not appeared as often all the way through the last dozen or so cards. If the looked-at-cards are simply replaced somewhere in the deck, this possibility is eliminated, so your final score will accurately reflect your telepathic abilities.

After a few runs, reverse it so that you are concentrating

on the colour and your partner is attempting to pick up the colour you are thinking about. You may find that you are better at sending than receiving, or vice versa.

Here is the same test made twice as hard. Instead of trying to transmit the colour of the card, transmit the suit - spades, hearts, clubs or diamonds. Change the deck you use for these tests frequently. During World War Two an American sailor discovered he was exceptionally good at this sort of test, even being able to name the actual card - three of clubs, and so on. His scores were so unbelievable that his shipmates arranged for him to be tested at a parapsychology laboratory. There he was a dismal failure. The reason was that he had always used the same deck of cards and unconsciously recognised certain flaws and marks on the cards. So, even though he thought he was doing it genuinely, it was not an example of ESP. So remember to use as many different decks of cards as you can.

Once you get really good at this, you can try and go for the name of the card. However, this is much more difficult and it would pay to work your way up to this by trying the next experiments first.

This is a good experiment as it helps you develop a number of skills at the same time. Give your partner a small object that has been in your possession for a long time and has some emotional meaning for you. A watch or an item of jewelry is ideal. Whilst you are out of the room have your friend hide the item. After he has done this return to the room and ask him to hold your left wrist between the thumb and first or second finger of his right hand. Ask him to think to himself the direction you should take to find the item. For instance, if it was straight ahead he is to think "move forwards". If it was to the left, he must think "turn to the left". Wait until you feel something, then move in that direction. Your friend is to think "stop", when you have moved far enough in one direction, then "turn right", "turn left" or whatever other command takes you in the right direction. Once you are close to the object, he must think "stop", followed by "raise your right hand. Feel behind the clock, etc." until you find the hidden item.

This may sound like a difficult and daunting test, and it may well be the first few times you try it. Remember that practice makes perfect, and with diligence you will be able to master this. This is actually known as "contact mind reading", as you are in physical contact with the other person. You may have seen Kreskin, for instance, finding his pay cheque in a theatre by using contact mind reading. A lot of people have achieved fame and fortune using contact mind reading alone, so it will certainly repay you many times the small amount of effort required to master it.

Here's an experiment which will let your creative abilities flower. Ask your friend to think of a simple picture, such as a house, a chair, a boat, the sun, etc. Sit opposite him, get into a relaxed state and tune into his mind. Don't hurry this test. It may take quite a few minutes before an image finds its way into your mind. Once you have it, take a pad and pencil and draw down what you pictured. Then check it out with what your friend was thinking.

You may prefer an alternative method. Ask your friend to draw a simple shape or design, and then try and duplicate it. This can be much more interesting. Your friend may be thinking of a box-shaped house, but in his drawing he may have included a row of flowers in front of the house. Your drawing may accurately duplicate the house, but you may have a strange squiggle in front. This is because you are picking up something from your friend, but it is vague as he is actually concentrating on the house rather than the flowers. This is very evidential of ESP at work. Of course, once you can duplicate simple designs, move progressively onto more complicated pictures.

There is a lot of material in this chapter. Don't be in a hurry to master it all. The experiments are designed to develop your psychic abilities progressively, so anything ignored or rushed over at this stage will only have to be repeated later. You will not master everything here overnight, but be familiar and comfortable with it all before starting the next chapter.

Remember to make a cassette tape to help your subconscious open itself to other people's thoughts.

# CHAPTER FOUR

# CLAIRVOYANCE

Now we are starting on something that will be of great practical use to you if you take up psychic work professionally. Clairvoyance is the name given to describe the ability to pick up information without using the normal senses. For instance, in one of the tests in the last chapter, you had a friend look at a playing card and then transmit the colour or suit to you. That is telepathy. If you were able to know what the colour and suit was without having anyone transmit the information to you, it is an example of clairvoyance. One major use of clairvoyance is in Psychometry, and that is so important that it will be dealt with separately in a later chapter.

Here is an interesting experiment. Find a small wooden box that can be locked. Your partner from the telepathy experiments is to ask someone to place some small object in the box and then to lock it. Neither your partner nor you are there whilst this is done, and it is better if you do not even know the person who has chosen what goes into the box. Your partner brings the box to you, and using your clairvoyant abilities you determine what is in the box.

Now, how do you do that? Firstly, be confident in your own mind that you can succeed at this experiment. Then relax completely and move your hands around the box, just a few centimetres away from its surface. You will probably experience a tingling sensation in your fingertips, and this is all to the good. Keep relaxed and be in no hurry. If after five or six minutes you have no idea what is inside, put the box away for about twenty four hours and then try again. If you have no success on this occasion, try the experiment again, but hold the box in your hands whilst attempting it. Your friend should try the experiment as well, but bear in mind that he knows the person who put the item into the box, so could have unconsciously picked up the thought telepathically. If he does get an impression, he is not to tell you what it is until you have an idea yourself.

This is not an easy test, but is one that can be useful in daily life. Imagine being able to pick up a sealed letter and know what is inside! That is actually easier to do than the same test with a wooden box. Try this test several times, using different people to load the box each time, if possible.

Persevere with this first test as it is a good exercise to develop your clairvoyant abilities. Whilst you are doing it you may want to try some of these easier experiments as well.

Take out your pack of playing cards again and try the experiment of determining if a card is red or black before you turn it over. Yes, this is virtually the same experiment we did in the previous chapter, but done with clairvoyance rather than telepathy. Remember to change decks regularly as explained earlier.

Here is a test using playing cards that is more interesting. Thoroughly mix the pack and then draw a card at random from the centre of the deck. Memorise this card. For the sake of description we will call it the four of hearts, but it could be any card at all. Replace this card somewhere in the deck before giving it a good shuffle. Cut the cards in to two, approximately even, piles. Relax and place a hand over each pile and try and determine which pile contains your chosen card (the four of hearts in our example). If you feel that your left hand is being drawn down to its pile, check through the cards to see if it contains your card.

Do this at least ten times, keeping a record of your successes. By chance alone, you should succeed five times out of ten. Don't be alarmed if you scored around five or lower. Just keep practicing until you can get it correct eight or more times out of ten. No psychic is correct all of the time, and if you can get eight right every time you do this test you are doing very well.

Once you have reached this level, try dividing the pack into four, then six or eight piles. This makes it much harder to succeed by chance alone, so makes a more evidential test of your abilities.

Here is another test along similar lines. Obtain about half a dozen empty plastic film cannisters. You want them all to be exactly the same. I obtained mine from one of the one hour film processing laboratories that appear to be everywhere nowadays. They collect them by the thousand, so will be only too pleased to give you as many as you want. Take a bag full and then sort out the ones that are most alike when you get home.

Borrow someone's wedding ring. Find a coin that weighs virtually the same as the ring. Get five of these coins. Line the cannisters on a table and have the tops beside them. You will also need a large paper bag. Turn your back on the cannisters, and have a friend place the ring in one of them and a coin in each of the others. The lid is placed on each and the sealed cannisters are placed into a paper bag. Shake the bag thoroughly. The reason for doing all of this behind your back was to eliminate the possibility of you seeing some small imperfection in the cannister which the ring went in to. Pour the six cannisters out on to the table. Relax, then pass your hands over each of the cannisters in turn, testing to see if your hands are drawn to any one in particular. Take your time and you will gradually feel something stronger emanating from one. This should be the one containing the ring. Again try this test several times, keeping a record of the number of successes.

Incidentally, I have a friend who is extremely good at this test, only she does it by a process of eliminating cannisters one at a time, until she is left with the one containing the ring. I personally prefer the first method as it is conceivably possible - though very unlikely - that my friend can detect the slight difference in weight between a coin and the ring. However, I mention it as you may find yourself being more successful with this method.

As a psychic, you may be asked to locate lost items, such as jewelry. Here is where clairvoyance comes into its own. You can not pick up the thought telepathically as no one knows where the missing item is. You will be able to do it, though, clairvoyantly. Simply relax, visualise the person who owns the lost item, then think about the missing article. Frequently you will get a flash of inspiration that the item is in a certain place. Check these feelings out. Most people rely too much on logic. By relaxing first, then visualising, you eliminate cold, hard logic and really flow with your feelings. This is the secret of being a true psychic - simply acting on your feelings. You won't be right all of the time, of course, but you will be correct enough of the time to please everyone you know who is looking for a missing item.

Whilst living in London many years ago, I had a friend who could always find a parking space whenever she wanted one. She simply used her clairvoyant abilities and "saw" the street in her mind's eye before turning into it. In her picture she saw the street, complete with parking spaces, if there were any. If you have ever tried to find parking in the middle of London you will appreciate how useful this psychic ability can be. You can, of course, do the same experiment wherever you live. Simply relax, whilst driving, and visualise the streets you are heading towards and see them in your mind. If you see a parking space, make use of it and congratulate yourself on making your ESP talents so practical. I use this at times, but find it best if I decide to use it before starting to look for a space. If I spend several minutes driving around trying to find parking and then decide to use my friend's system, it is that much harder as I have managed to frustrate myself, making it more difficult to relax.

Here is an interesting experiment, but not one that you can always verify. Everywhere you go you will find cupboards and drawers. Next time you visit somewhere for the first time take note of any cupboards or drawers, and, if you get a moment, relax and visualise what is inside the cupboard or drawer. You will not always be able to check your accuracy, of course, but you will surprise yourself in time with how accurate you can be when you are allowed to check on the contents.

I had an interesting experience one time with this experiment. I was visiting a lady who was recovering from a bad fall. She was bed ridden, so I offered to make the afternoon tea. As I couldn't find the teapot in her kitchen, I simply visualised different cupboards until I found it, not in the kitchen at all, but in the dining room. I made the tea and carried it in to the bedroom, and my hostess was amazed as I had made the tea in a teapot she had not been able to find in years! She had assumed it had been completely lost. Yet by visualising cupboards I was able to find it.

This is another experiment in clairvoyance. Some people call this test "remote viewing". The evening before you are to go somewhere new, sit back, relax and visualise the place you will be visiting the next day. Suppose you have an appointment to see a dentist you have not visited before. Try and imagine his waiting roonm and surgery. Obviously, he will have somewhere for people to wait and he'll have the usual array of drills and other paraphernalia. You will see all this, of course, but try and see everything else - the layout of the office, the type of seating, the names of magazines to look at whilst waiting, the pictures, if any, on the walls, the presence or absence of a bowl of goldfish, and so on. You may even visualise the dentist and his nurse. The following day you can check yourself for accuracy.

I find that tests like this which can be done in daily life are often the best as far as developing one's abilities are concerned. Tests, such as the ones with playing cards, are good to begin with but can become boring. Once this happens one's ESP ability tends to decrease. Tests which can be done in the real world can seldom be duplicated, but, because you are really involved in them, can be that much more rewarding as far as psychic development is concerned.

We will cover more on clairvoyance in the chapter on Psychometry. If you practised all of the tests in this chapter you will find the tests in the Psychometry section that much easier. I hope you can see, and are beginning to prove to yourself, how practical and useful ESP can be in everyday life.

## CHAPTER FIVE

# PRECOGNITION

Many people who believe in Telepathy and Clairvoyance still find it hard to accept the possibility of seeing into the future. This has always seemed strange to me as often I get an impression, and afterwards find it hard to say whether it came through telepathy, clairvoyance or precognition - or even, perhaps, a mixture of all three.

I think the reason many people refuse to accept the possibility of seeing into the future, is that many people have had predictions of tragic events, usually relating to people close to them, so close their minds to the whole subject. It seems that the more horrible or diabolical the event the greater the energies created, and these can be picked up by people close to the affected parties, even though they may not usually be psychic.

The ability to see into the future has been believed in and accepted virtually since mankind managed to stand on two feet. The oldest piece of writing in existence is on Numerology (often used for looking into the future) and is on the back of a tortoise shell in China. One of my ambitions is to see it for myself.

This ability to see into the future is a vital skill if you are to become a professional psychic, as most of your clients will come to you because they want to know about something that has not yet occurred.

I find it very helpful when looking into someone's future if I think about the famous analogy of a passenger on a train. He is sitting in the train, looking at the fields, and the present is what he can see out his window. Yet someone in a plane flying above can see this train passenger's past, present and future. I imagine that I'm the one in the plane and my client is sitting in the train.

The whole concept of time is impossible to define. Is the present this hour, this minute or this second? Even physicists argue about time and what it is. However, look at the passenger in the train again. Isn't the person flying overhead transcending this train passenger's time to see part of his future? That is all we have to do to see into the future - transcend time for a short while.

You already know most of the steps to achieve this. Firstly, go to your special place and relax. Next, imagine that you and every living thing in the world are somehow attached by invisible cords, that everything is interconnected. Now think about tomorrow and what you will be doing.

You won't need much precognitive ability to determine most of it. Presumably, you'll have to get up in the morning and have breakfast. You may have to go to work and spend eight or nine hours doing something that hopefully you enjoy. After that you come home, have a meal, possibly watch television and go to bed. You certainly don't have to be a fortune teller to deduce that! However, whilst imagining tomorrow take note of the little things you see. Odd words and phrases, the person sitting next to you on the bus, someone away from work, and so on. Make the whole picture as vivid and complete as you can.

Once you open your eyes again, jot down the important or

unusual things you noticed in your visualisation. Think no more about it until the following night when you compare what actually happened with what you envisaged. You may be pleasantly surprised that many of the things you noted down actually happened, proving to you that you can actually transcend time.

This test is especially useful if you have a completely free day ahead and do not know what you are going to do in it. Simply project yourself forward to that day and see what will eventuate.

You also have the power to change your future, of course. If you want a raise at work, for example, relax in your chair, close your eyes and "see" your boss coming over to you and giving you a raise. See it so vividly that you can not imagine it not happening. Do this every night, and at odd moments during the day if you get any spare time. Before many days pass, your boss may well come over and say that he had a strange feeling that he should give you a raise. Once this has happened you will have demonstrated your ability to not only see into the future, but to change it.

As a psychic, you will be asked to look into the future of other people. There are a number of ways of doing this using Palmistry, Astrology, Tarot Cards, etc. and we will go into some of these later on. Here we are concerned with looking into the future simply using your natural senses.

It is not necessary to have the other person with you when you do this exercise, though you must be able to form a strong impression of them. You may want to hold something belonging to them, or to have a photograph of them, but although these may help, they are not essential. Relax as usual, then imagine yourself being interconnected with everyone else. Once you reach this stage, imagine yourself being totally in tune with the person concerned. Visualise them so strongly that you can see them in your mind's eye. See yourself being as one with them. Hold this image for as long as you can, and then let yourself move into the future using their eyes.

Using this method, you can look into the future of anyone - even total strangers, providing you can visualise them clearly enough. I have a friend who writes a psychic column for a newspaper. He uses this method to obtain all of his information.

There are other tests you can do, also, but they lack the emotional power of the ones already mentioned. Here are a few using your by now well-used pack of cards.

Think about your pack of cards and visualise what the top card of the deck will be once you have thoroughly shuffled them. Write the name of this card down. Mix the cards and turn over the top one to see if your prediction was correct. After doing this a few times, you can vary it by predicting what the third card down from the top will be, or the tenth, or the fortieth - just whatever number you choose.

Once you get good at this, you can jot down the names of the first four or five cards and see what result you get.

Here is an experiment you can do with your friend from the previous chapters. Think about what he will do, if you ask him to do something out of character. He may thump his chest and imitate a gorilla, he may make Red Indian type war whoops, he may slump into a chair and refuse to do anything - he could do anything. Write down your prediction of what you think he will do, and then invite him over. Once he arrives tell him about your prediction and ask him to do something out of character. Do not think about the actions you wrote down. Simply watch and see what he does. If you succeed your friend will be highly impressed; if you fail your friend will understand as he will have been working along with you anyway. This test can be great fun. The only problem with it is that your friend may be picking up the right action cues from you clairvoyantly, even if you are not consciously thinking of what you want him to do, so it is not as good a test of precognition as the first ones mentioned.

This is a good test, although it may not always be easy to get verification. Choose someone you know well by sight, but who is not a friend. Go to your usual spot, relax and visualise this person. Then, using his eyes, move into the future until you come to something different or exciting. It is unlikely to be overdramatic - it could be a good night out or some unexpected news. Write this down, and a day or two after the event has occurred ask this person if they enjoyed seeing such-and-such a film, or whatever it was that happened. You will enjoy seeing the surprised look appear on their face as they ask you how on earth you knew they had done that!

Be careful with your timing on this experiment. I tried it once with a man who lived next door to me. When I asked him how he had enjoyed a certain film, he looked at me as if I was mad, and said that he had heard bad comments about it and would never, ever go to see it, and certainly had not already done so. I was a little surprised as my vision had been extremely strong, but shrugged it off as being a mistake. A few days later this man rang me and told me had seen the film, and that I should go as it was excellent. It turned out that his son had come home unexpectedly from overseas and had taken his parents out to see the film. So my original prediction had been correct, but I was a few days out in my timing!

Timing can be difficult. Twenty years ago in England I knew an extremely gifted psychic lady. She was kept very busy with a regular clientele of satisfied clients, but every so often she would tell a client in great detail what was going to happen, only to have the client tell her that it had already occurred! What she thought was in the future, was often in the past. I lost contact with this lady many years ago, and have often wondered if she managed to solve the problem of timing. Incidentally, it did not affect her credibility - rather the reverse. Her clients would be impressed with the accuracy and detail of her descriptions, which made them that much more attentive when she was describing things yet to come.

So be careful when predicting the future for someone. You may be certain that something will happen next Wednesday, but unless you have discovered over a period of time that your timing is excellent, it might be better to say, "Such-and-such will happen next week, probably around Wednesday." This way, you will be correct, even if it happens on Tuesday or Friday.

There are ways to check your timing using systems such as Numerology, which we will go into later on, but are out of the scope of this chapter.

Don't forget that you can make enormous changes in your own life with precognition. Relax and run through a preview of what lies ahead for you. You will see things that will please you, but also things that you would like to avoid or change. You have the power to do all of this. Look at the stages which are not so pleasant, and think how you can alter them. Be realistic, and make any necessary changes. If you do this you can alter your whole future.

I taught this to a young man who came to me shortly after he had been in trouble with the law. On looking ahead for him I saw continued trouble and ultimate imprisonment. He appeared to be on a totally self-destructive course. He took no notice of what I said, so on an impulse I taught him how to relax and suggested he go through his own life in the peace of his own home, and see what it revealed. He was skeptical, but returned a few days later wanting definite pointers on how he could change his life. I am pleased to say that he did change his life, and has almost finished an accountancy degree, so the future is looking very bright for him. I hope any necessary changes in your life are not quite so dramatic, but that you take whatever actions are required to get you onto the right path.

## CHAPTER SIX

# PSYCHOMETRY

You may be wondering why this chapter has been placed after the Precognition one, rather than immediately after Clairvoyance. The reason is that Psychometry is an aspect of clairvoyance, but you will usually be using it in a precognitive way. In other words, you may be holding someone's ring and telling them about the past, present *and* future. So you are in a better position to study this chapter now, after working on the tests in the last two chapters.

Psychometry is the ability to sense vibrations from objects, and derives from two Greek words - *psyche*, 'the soul', and *metron*, 'a measure' - literally being able to measure the soul of things.

Initially, you may find it hard to sense anything at all, but persevere as you will find this an extremely useful skill in daily life. For instance, if someone asked you to sign a contract, you could hold the piece of paper in your hands for a few moments and sense as to whether or not to sign it. If you were planning to buy a beautiful object, you could hold or touch it to determine if the seller was telling the truth about it. These are but two examples of the types of things you will be able to do after you have mastered this chapter.

Here is a test you can do with your partner. Get him to collect a number of small items - five or six would be plenty - all of which have belonged to him for a long while. Then to add to this collection an item which belongs to someone else. All of these objects should be items not known by you. Have them placed together in a paper bag, and bring them out one at a time. Ignore what the object is. Just sense it with your fingers. I find it easiest to relax completely and imagine my fingers being full of psychic energy. That way, when I touch anything, I get an immediate psychometric response. Hold each object for several seconds to see what feelings come through, then place it on the table. Go through all the items the same way, to see what comes to your mind. You may be surprised at how strong some of the feelings are. Say out loud any particular sensation or feeling you receive, so your partner can verify it later. However, he is not to say anything at all whilst the experiment is in progress. When you have been through all the items, one of them should have felt slightly different to the others, and this will be the item your friend borrowed from someone else.

If you are correct first time, and the chances are high that you will be, if you have conscientiously done all the previous exercises in this book, you can then return to your partner's belongings and see what other feelings you receive. After this, pick up the borrowed item and see what you can gain from holding it.

At first you may come up with only a few words, but in time, as you develop your psychometric capabilities you may find yourself talking rapidly for several minutes! I have a friend in America who does full sixty minutes readings purely by psychometrizing something belonging to the person. If you are prepared to work at it, you will be able to do this as well.

Here is an interesting variant to the first experiment. Your friend will this time have to find several objects that have led peaceful existences, plus an item that has been involved in an accident or disaster of some sort. For instance, in my own classes I use a watch that belonged to someone who was killed in a car accident. Even now, twenty years after the event, it is easy for my students to pick up that it had been involved in a tragedy. You may find this version easier than the first, as some items that have been involved in a disaster of some sort virtually scream their history to you.

As you are obviously interested in the psychic world, you are probably familiar with crystals. They are usually used for healing purposes or for chakra purification, but they are also very useful in developing psychometric talents. Buy several crystals, feminine ones if possible. (These are the 'milky' ones, and are much better for psychic work than the masculine, or clear, crystals.) These crystals should be about two inches long, and plain quartz is ideal for this experiment. If they are very alike, you should stick a small sticker on each one, after washing them, to aid identification later. Have your partner wash them all in a saline solution and let the crystals dry in sunlight. After this, he is to take one crystal at random, and hold it in his closed palms, all the while sending 'hateful' thoughts to it. He may say out loud, "I hate you. You are horrible and disgusting. You fill me with loathing, etc." After ten minutes of this, he is to put that crystal down, and choose another one at random. This one he is to fill with loving thoughts. Holding it the same way, he should say something like this. "You are beautiful and precious. You are full of love and tenderness. You are sympathetic and caring, etc." Now he is to bring them all in to you, as you must not be present whilst the preparation takes place.
Pick up the crystals one at a time and see what feelings you get. Crystals are extremely sensitive, so you should have

no trouble at all in identifying the one full of love and the one full of hate. After this experiment wash the crystals again in a saline solution to remove these vibrations.

You can do other tests with these crystals as well. Have your partner entrust a crystal to a small child for a few days. Then have it mixed up with the others. Pick them up one at a time, and see if you can pick up the carefree enthusiasm and playfulness of youth in the one the child had.

Try the same experiment in different ways. One crystal could be left in a hospital ward for a few days. It could be left in a night club, a kindergarten, the home of an optimist, the home of a pessimist - and so on. Crystals pick up vibrations extremely easily, and you will find them very helpful in aiding your development.

You may be interested to learn that there is at least one parapsychology laboratory where psychometry is being tested all the time. This is the Parapsychological Institute at the Rijksuniversiteitte in Utrecht, Holland, and here they use psychometry to help the police solve difficult crimes.

There is also a large library of documented psychometry successes. One man who took a great interest in the subject last century was a Professor William Denton. He wrote three books on the subject, all of which are still available today. Most of his experiments were done with his sister, an extremely gifted psychic. Professor Denton's subject was geology, so a number of the objects he gave his sister to psychometrize were geological in origin. For instance, here is the reading she gave on being handed a piece of lava from Hawaii:

Firstly, she was seized with a feeling of terror that lasted for an hour. Then she gave this reading. "I see the ocean and ships are sailing on it. This must be an island, for water is all around. Now I am turned from where I see the vessels, and am looking at something most terrific. It seems as if an ocean of fire were pouring over a precipice, and boiling as it pours. The sight permeates my whole being, and inspires me with terror. I see it flow into the ocean and the water boils intensely."

Here is another reading she gave on being handed a piece of a mastoden tooth: "My impression is that it is part of some monstrous animal, probably part of a tooth. I feel like a perfect monster, with heavy legs, unwieldy head, and very large body. I go down to a shallow stream to drink. I can hardly speak, my jaws are so heavy. I feel like getting down on all fours. What a noise comes through the wood. I have an impulse to answer it. My ears are very large and leathery, and I can almost fancy they flap my face as I move my head. There are some older ones than I. It seems, too, so out of keeping to be talking with these heavy jaws. They are dark brown, as if they had been completely tanned. There is one old fellow, with large tusks, that looks very tough. I see several young ones; in fact, there is a whole herd."

I have given these readings in full, as they demonstrate very vividly how Mrs Cridge actually became a mastoden. All of her senses were actively involved. She found it hard to talk, she felt an impulse to answer a sound, she saw around her the rest of the herd. With the first example, she felt a sense of terror, after gradually picking up a description of the island.

When you hold something to psychometrize you must completely relax, so that you can not only sense the vibrations, but feel them in every part of you, so that you in fact become part of the scene - just as Mrs Cridge actually became a mastoden whilst giving the reading.

Some psychometrists seem to take this almost too far. One famous medium of Victorian times, Bessie Williams, used to work with a doctor, aiding his diagnosis by psychometry. After a while she had to give it up as she kept getting the symptoms of all the illnesses she diagnosed. A modern day Dutch psychometrist, Frau Lotte Plaat, found it impossible to go into the British Museum as all the items shouted out their histories to her.

I hope that you don't take it quite this far, but you can see that it is possible to develop your psychometric abilities a long way. Keep practising, make a cassette for yourself on psychometry to listen to when you relax, and your skills will steadily develop.

## CHAPTER SEVEN

# PSYCHOKINESIS

Psychokinesis (PK for short) means mind over matter, in other words, the ability to influence an object or event by using the powers of the mind alone. The ability of Ingo Swann to slow down the breakdown rate of radio-active material is a good example of PK in action. Uri Geller's spoon bending could be another.

PK stands a little apart from the other main areas of ESP. Telepathy, clairvoyance and precognition are all very much interconnected, and it is not always easy to determine which was used in every case. However, there is no doubt with PK. If you are able to make a pencil stand on end, simply by using the power of your mind, you are very obviously using your psychokinetic abilities.

This may sound like a rather useless ability, and one that you will be unlikely to ever need. At one stage I was able to make flash bulbs pop by simply concentrating on them. One day whilst doing it my nose started to bleed and continued off and on for three days, so I have not attempted it since. This was an example of PK, but a rather silly one - much like bending spoons. So a number of PK experiments are rather trivial, but there are also instances where PK ability could not be more important.

Take psychic, or spiritual, healing, for example. Usually this is done by the laying on of hands, so is an example of

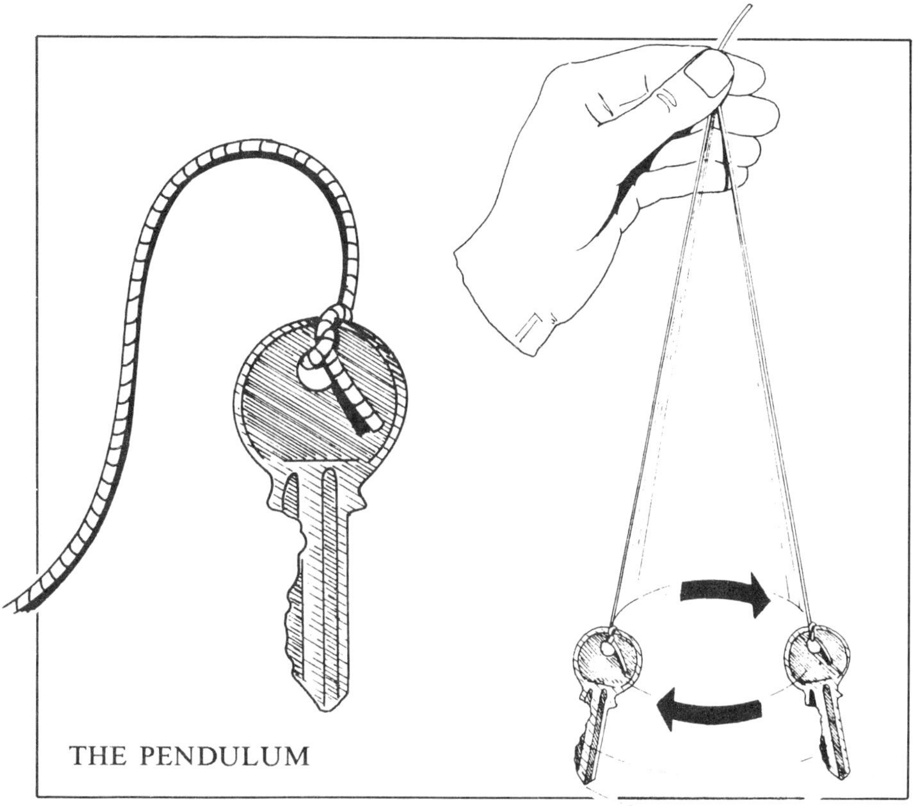

THE PENDULUM

PK in action. The mind of one person is creating a physical effect in the body of someone else, and if this aids in curing the person, it is an extremely important and practical use of PK. We will talk more about spiritual healing later on.

Have you ever tried to determine the sex of an unborn baby by using a ring on the end of a string? This has been a popular activity for centuries, and is one small part of the use of a pendulum. You can buy yourself a good pendulum from any psychic bookshop, but it is just as easy to make your own. Simply tie a ring or light key on the end of a piece of thin string about eight or nine inches long. Suspend the pendulum by passing the string over your first finger and holding it in place with your thumb.

Let the pendulum hang an inch or two above a table and go through your relaxation exercises. Then concentrate your mind on willing the pendulum to sway backwards and forwards. Within a minute or so, the pendulum will sway to and fro. Whilst it is still moving, start concentrating on the pendulum going round and round in a circle. You will find the pendulum will gradually stop moving to and fro and will start to go round and round. Once it is going in a fine circular fashion, will it to go back and forth again. It will obey your thoughts and stop revolving. After several minutes of this, say to yourself that the pendulum is tired and will it to stop. Within a minute it will stop completely.

After doing this test successfully you will have done your first exercise in PK, as it was your mind that influenced the pendulum to act as it did.

Now let's take that same test a little further. On a large piece of paper draw the floor plan of your home, clearly showing each room. Have your partner place an object in one of the rooms. He is to tell you what the object is, but is to take no further part in the experiment. In fact, it would be better if he left the house whilst you try this test as you do not want to pick up any information from him, either telepathically or clairvoyantly. So, in front of you you have the layout of your home. Pick up the pendulum, relax, and ask the pendulum to tell you what room the object is in. Hold it over each room in turn, asking it to move backwards and forwards in the rooms that do not contain the item, but round and round in the room it is in. Be patient, and give the pendulum sufficient time to change direction when it is hanging over the correct room. Once you have the pendulum swinging round and around in one room, deliberately move it into an adjacent room to see if it returns to swinging to and fro. Move it back again to see if it starts moving in a circular direction, and then check your findings. You should be able to find the object in the room indicated by your pendulum.

What if you live in a one room apartment? Simply make a large drawing of the room and include all the furniture. Ask your partner to place the object somewhere in the room, and then, using your pendulum see if you can find the correct spot in the room. You can even do this when you are away from home. Have your friend place the item somewhere in your house, and then go over the floorplan with your pendulum wherever you happen to be. You will find that distance has no bearing on your success.

Can you see how useful this test will be if you are looking for a lost item? Simply use the pendulum to find the room, and then if the item is very small, use a large drawing of the room to locate the exact spot. With a missing item, you can of course walk through the house, testing with the pendulum as you go.

Now we will make the test even harder. Obtain a large street map of your local area. Have your friend go off to any place shown on the map. Have him decide where he is going to go after leaving the house, so that you don't read his mind before he leaves. At a previously agreed time, go over the map street by street using your pendulum. At one point it will start to go round in circles. Check, as in the previous example, and then go to the place to pick up your partner.

From here you can widen your horizons almost indefinitely. Think about someone who you have not seen for a while. See if you can locate where they are now by using your pendulum over a map of the area. Make sure to check your results, even when you do not appear to have any result at all. The person you are thinking about may not have been in the area covered by your map at the time you did the test.

Once you have developed this ability, you will be able to use it to help locate missing people. This is one of the things people will come to you about if you take up psychic work professionally.

You may have heard of table tilting or apports. These both became popular about a hundred years ago in the heyday of the seance. Several people would place their hands on a table and will it to move. This is an example of the minds of several people influencing an object. Apports are not so easy to explain. They are things that appear unexpectedly, usually in the darkness of a seance room. When the lights are turned back on the sitters may find a bunch of flowers in the middle of the table that had materialised during the seance. It could be a ring, a scarf - virtually anything. Sometimes it may even be objects belonging to the sitters that had previously been lost.

Scientists are actively involved in testing for PK, and are particularly interested in the area of making things move. You may recall many years ago seeing a Russian woman called Nelya Kulagina moving objects using simply the power of her mind. In some cases, she could actually make small objects levitate for a short time. In one test at Stanford Research Institute, Ingo Swann, who we have mentioned before, was challenged to see if he could alter the flow of recordings coming from a magnetometer. He promptly succeeded, but the physicist in charge was skeptical and claimed it was caused by coincidence. He would only believe it if Ingo Swann could stop the ripple effect. Swann promptly did exactly that for several seconds.

Poltergeist activities are another form of PK, and I hope you will never encounter this for yourself, as the damage caused by poltergeists can be considerable.

So you see, there are a number of areas in PK. Here we are concentrating on the practical areas, so that you will be able to use them yourself. Helping to locate a missing person is an extremely useful ability, and apart from helping to heal the sick, is probably the most important PK skill.

We will only touch on psychic healing here, as it is something you will learn best by watching other psychic healers at work. What I find fascinating is that each psychic healer has his own special way of working. For instance, one lady I know has her patients lying naked under a sheet. She then holds her hands, palms down, about six inches above the sheet and moves them up and down the length of the body. She gets good results, but so does another friend of mine. All he does is whisper into the patient's ear. I have no idea what he says, as the patient has to keep it secret, but it seems to work. Other healers work in more traditional ways, by simply placing their hands on the patient's head. Many healers use crystals of different sorts, some like to have incense in the room, others need to perform a brief ritual before they start work. As I said, everyone seems to employ his own method.

However, they all have one thing in common. Without exception, they believe they are capable of healing the person they are working on. Some believe that they are actually the cause of the healing, others insist that they are simply a channel - but they all believe they can do it.

I think the best way to learn psychic healing is to observe

other people doing it, and to attend classes, if possible. However, here is a test you can try to see if healing is likely to be your forte.

Next time someone you know has a headache ask them to sit down on a chair, place their feet on the floor, and relax. By now you should know your relaxation procedure by heart, so simply say it out loud as the other person relaxes. Once they have relaxed to the best of their ability, place both your hands firmly on the other person's head. Believe that you are capable of stopping the other person's headache, and will it to happen. You may find it easier if you talk calmly and quietly as you do this. "You are completely relaxed and at peace. The pain that has been troubling you is going away, it is fading away and will vanish completely in the next few minutes. You are feeling fine and relaxed and rested. The pain is going and you are feeling at peace with the world." Keep on saying comments like this for several minutes until the pain has gone.

Always remember, though, that no pain occurs without a reason. It is possible to make a pain go away by using these methods, but you may not be removing the original cause. So, should the pain recur send the person to a good doctor. I personally feel that all psychic healing should be done alongside more orthodox methods.

We have covered a lot of material in this chapter. Psychokinesis is a complete study in itself, but not all of it is of practical use. By all means try and make objects levitate or spoons bend, but devote most of your attention to pendulum skills and healing.

## CHAPTER EIGHT

# A PAUSE FOR BREATH

You have accomplished a great deal in the last half dozen chapters. This one is to give you a break to evaluate your progress. By now, you should be able to relax at will, whenever you want, and wherever you happen to be. You will be capable of picking up other people's thoughts, and will also be adept at transmitting your thoughts to others. You will be able to get glimpses of future events, and find missing people. Your clairvoyant abilities will have increased, particularly in the area of psychometry, and you will be wondering "where do we go from here?"

Everything we have covered so far will be useful to you in daily life, and you should be finding your life becoming richer in every way as a result of these experiments. Your confidence will have increased as your psychic talents gradually unfolded. Actually, you already have most of the knowledge you need to become a successful psychic. If you are going to become a psychometrist who helps the police solve crimes, you could stop reading at this point, as the rest of this book goes into the techniques and skills needed to become a psychic reader.

Most people, when they go to a psychic, expect to be told about their past, present and future. If you set yourself up as a psychic consultant you will be using clairvoyance and precognition all the time. You may also use telepathy, to pick up problems that your client is thinking about. In fact, everything we have covered so far will be useful and practical to you.

However, it is unlikely that you will be able to pick up enough information using these alone to give your client a full and satisfactory reading. To do this you will need some sort of 'crutch'; something else to base your reading on. It may be palmistry, numerology, tarot cards, rune stones - in fact virtually anything at all, as long as it appeals to you. For my own readings I usually use a combination of palmistry and numerology. However, at times, I also use astrology, tarot cards and rune stones. For years I used a crystal ball in my readings. If you know anything about astrology, you can see that I'm a typical Sagittarian, trying to learn about everything! All you need do is become good at one 'crutch'.

Think about the different possibilities. If you have had a reading done in the past and were absolutely fascinated with the beautiful cards in the tarot deck, you may decide that tarot cards are just the thing for you. Maybe you saw someone using a crystal ball and would love to have one of your own. In that case I'd certainly recommend that you try scrying. You may be highly practical and decide that as everyone else in your area is using tarot cards you will use rune stones, or the cartouche, or gem stones. You should also bear in mind that it will take years of study to become a competent astrologer, but you can learn the basics of tarot card reading in a few weeks. This is because you have already put the background work in. It is possible to be a competent tarot card reader, for example, by diligently studying many books on the subject and practising, but you can only become a fantastic reader if you use the cards, but also use telepathy, clairvoyance and precognition. This is what makes the difference, and is the reason why you will be good at whatever 'crutch' you decide to use, because you will also be utilising all the skills you have developed so far.

It is impossible for me to suggest which of the psychic arts would be right for you, but to help you make up your mind, the next few chapters contain the basics of a few of the more popular of them. Use these chapters to give you a guide before selecting the one that appeals the most.

## CHAPTER NINE

# NUMEROLOGY

Numerology is one of the oldest of the occult sciences. In fact the oldest piece of writing in existence is written on the back of a tortoise shell and is on numerology. Numerology was brought 'up-to-date' some 2,600 years ago by Pythagoras, a man I'm sure you will remember from your school days.

Numerology uses the numbers one to nine, as well as eleven and twenty two. These last two are known as Master numbers, giving the person with them much more power and capability than someone without them. Many people consider that someone with an 11 or 22 as one of their main numbers is an "old soul", in other words, has been through many previous incarnations. However, it is not necessary to believe in reincarnation to become a good numerologist.

The most important number in numerology is called the Life Path, and it denotes the person's purpose in life. We work this number out by adding up all the numbers in the full date of birth in a little sum like this:

```
  27
   6
1955
----
1988, and 1+9+8+8=26, and 2+6=8
```

This person, born on the 27th of June, 1955, has a Life Path number of 8. The answer of the sum created by using the person's day, month and year of birth is gradually reduced to a single digit, unless we end up with 11 or 22. Try this one for yourself: 29/2/1944. The correct answer is 22, a Master number. Try this one: 12/9/1946. Did you end up with a 5?

Once you have done these, work out the Life Path numbers of the people in your family, so that you can refer to them as we go through the meanings of each number. Always work out the number in the way shown above. The reason for this is that it is possible to lose a Master number by simply stringing the numbers out in a line and adding them up that way. Try it with the date shown above - 29/2/1944 - and you will see what I mean.

***Meanings of the different Life Path numbers***

1. This is the number of individuation and independence. Someone with a Life Path of 1 needs to learn to stand on their own two feet and to become independent, and ultimately a leader. It is sometimes a lonely path, but it leads to ultimate success.

2. This is the number of the diplomat, the peacemaker, the go-between. This person needs someone else to feel complete, so would always prefer to be married rather than single. Someone on this path is likely to be the power behind the throne, rather than the leader. Consequently, he may not always receive credit for everything he does. This is a highly intuitive number, so people on this path are naturally psychic.

3. People on this path need to express themselves in some way, ideally creatively. This can come in a variety of ways

- usually talking! - but could well come through singing, dancing, art, music, writing, and so on. It is a light-hearted number, so people on this path are likely to be popular and fun to be with. Unfortunately, this number often lacks motivation.

4. This is the number of system and order. People on this path need to be well-organised, and to work within the limits they find themselves in. Many people on this path get frustrated with the situation they find themselves in, so try and get out of it. This never provides much satisfaction, and their greatest success comes once they stop battering their heads against the limits they find, and work within clearly defined limits.

5. This is the number of freedom and change. People on this path are restless and versatile. They are likely to be good at everything they attempt, but never stick long to any one activity. Consequently, they can often be rolling stones or 'jack-of-all-trades'. These people work best with room around them and something exciting to look forward to. They need to learn to use their time constructively and wisely, rather than waste time.

6. This is the number of home and family responsibility. These people are often responsible for more than their fair share, but are generally positive and enthusiastic. Their greatest happiness comes out of family activities, so are usually married. As this is one of the humanitarian numbers, people on this path often go into careers such as teaching and social work, where their caring outlook can be utilised.

7. This is the number of introspection and wisdom, so can be a lonely path at times. People on this path appear to be on a slightly different wavelength to others, so don't always

find it easy to make close friends. Over a lifetime, they gradually grow in knowledge and wisdom, generally building up a strong faith in the process.

8. This is the number of materialism. People on this path have definite material needs, and will work hard to achieve their goals. Once they have succeeded in this, they are happy to turn around and give parts of it away - but they need to achieve their goals, modest or enormous, first. People on this path should be careful not to be overly stubborn or rigid.

9. This is the number of the humanitarian. 6 is also a humanitarian number but is usually concerned with people close to them; the 9 is concerned with humanity in general. This is a giving number, so people on this path often resent the necessity of forever giving - they would like to be able to take, just occasionally. People on this path are sensitive, caring people, but need to learn to stand up for themselves.

11. This is the first of the Master numbers. It stands for illumination and inspiration. People on this path are highly intuitive and have the ability to come up with ideas that can benefit humanity as a whole. Unfortunately, not all of their ideas are practical, so they work best with someone who can both encourage them and help them keep their feet on the ground. Once using their considerable powers in a positive way, they can achieve any goal they set.

22. This Master number is known as the master builder. It can take the ideas of the 11, and make them practical and workable. People on this path can achieve anything they set their minds on, and usually like to do things on a large scale. Unfortunately, both 11 and 22 are hampered with a degree of nervous tension which can work against their best interests, particularly early on in life.

Do you recognise yourself and other members of your family in that list? The Life Path is the most important number in Numerology, but is a little like the Sun sign in astrology in that it divides all of humanity in to eleven groups. The other numbers gradually help build up the complete picture.

The next most important number is called the Expression, and represents the person's natural abilities. This is worked out by turning the person's full name at birth into numbers. For this, we need the following chart:

| 1 | 2 | 3 | 4 | 5 | 6 | 7 | 8 | 9 |
|---|---|---|---|---|---|---|---|---|
| A | B | C | D | E | F | G | H | I |
| J | K | L | M | N | O | P | Q | R |
| S | T | U | V | W | X | Y | Z | |

When we write out the person's name, we write it in full, using the maiden name in the case of a woman, and we put the vowels above the name and the consonants below. The reason for this is that the third most important number is derived from the vowels. There is one exception to putting the vowels above and the consonants below, and that is with the letter "y". If it is pronounced, as in the name "Yolande" it is called a consonant, but if it is not pronounced, as in "Henry" or "Kay", it is classed as being a vowel.

Let's try a name.

```
    6          13/4        7
    1  5       1  57       6  1
CHARLES  STANLEY  THOMAS
38   93  1  12  53      28  4   1
  24/6         11          15/6
```

As you can see in this name, I have turned all the letters into numbers, then reduced them to a single digit. Note the "11" under the name "Stanley". 11, being a Master number, does not get reduced. Also note that the "y" in "Stanley" is classed as being a vowel.

Once we have done all of this, we simply add up all the numbers to arrive at Charles' Expression number.

6+4+7+6+11+6=40, and 4+0=4

Charles has an Expression number of 4, and that means that he is naturally good at the characteristics of the number 4. He would be hard working, well organised and capable of establishing order out of chaos.

The third number is called the Soul Urge, or the Heart's Desire. This is arrived at by adding up the value of the vowels. In Charles case, his Soul Urge is:

6+4+7=17, and 1+7=8

With a Soul Urge of 8, Charles would have definite material needs which have to be satisfied. Consequently, he is probably good at coming up with money-making ideas. He is fortunate in having a 4 Expression, as that means he is prepared to put the hard work in to make his ideas work.

The fourth most important number is derived from the person's day of birth. Let's assume that Charles was born on the 5th June, 1954. This means that he has a Life Path of 3 and a day of birth of 5.

Let's put all of these four numbers together. Charles has a Life Path of 3, an Expression of 4, a Soul Urge of 8 and a birthday of 5. The numbers go in descending order of importance, so Charles' Life Path number of 3 is the most important and the 5 of his day of birth the least important.

Somehow, Charles has to balance and, hopefully, harmonise the energies of all of these numbers. With a Life Path of 3 he is bound to be a sociable, conversational type of person who finds it easy to get along with others. However, both 4 and 8 can be stubborn numbers, so he may get offside with people sometimes by being too fixed in his approach. The 5 shows that he needs a lot of variety in his life, and possibly prefers being out of doors to being stuck in an office all day - the more room the better for a 5. How can he satisfy all of these different sides of his nature? Well, he could use the 3, 4 and 8 in a business venture of some sort. The 3 would make him a good salesman, the 4 shows that he doesn't mind hard work, and the 8 indicates that he will do well out of it. But he still needs to satisfy the 5. If he chose a business that allowed him space and variety, he could satisfy this as well. He could become a travel agent and travel overseas regularly, he could become a commission salesman, which would have him out and about; if he is sports-minded, he could set up a tennis coaching school, or something like that. He may even take up some form of entertainment as a career, using mainly the 3, but also the 4, 5 and 8.

Unfortunately, most people find it hard to satisfy all of their numbers. Charles, for instance, might be using just the 3 and the 8, making his living in a lazy, underhand manner, perhaps as a con man. His verbal skills assure success in that area, particularly with the 8 to back it up. If he made his living that way, he would be using the 4 in an negative manner, by being lazy rather than hard-working. He may make money this way, but would never feel really happy, as he would be aware all the time that he was not using his abilities as he should.

He may be using the 4 alone, and become a hard working, dissatisfied drudge. In this case he would carry an enormous chip on his shoulder and would forever be beating his head against the brick wall we mentioned earlier.

For Charles to be really happy, he needs to find for himself a career that uses as many of the numbers as possible. Say, he manages to satisfy the 3, 4 and 8. What about the 5? Well it would have to be utilised somehow, and Charles would probably have many satisfying, probably slightly unusual, hobbies. He could save his money each year and take an overseas holiday, which would certainly satisfy the 5, at least temporarily.

Can you see how we have built up a picture of the imaginary Charles, just by looking at his four main numbers? If he was sitting in front of you, you would be able to use your psychic abilities as well, and this background information derived from the numbers would provide an excellent starting point for a full reading.

We can also use Numerology to see how Charles will find the next few years.

To do this, all we do is add Charles' month and day of birth and add it to the current year. For instance, to find out how Charles will fare in 1988, we add up:

5 (day) + 6 (month) + 1+9+8+8 (current year) = 35, and 3+5=8

Charles is in an 8 Personal Year.

The years follow the numbers one to nine, so Charles will be having a money year in 1988. Let's look at these a little more closely.

1 year. This is a good year for starting new projects, as you will be full of enthusiasm and energy. Anything begun now lasts for a long time. It is a year of new beginnings.

2 year. A year for consolidating what was begun in the previous year. A good year for close relationships (2 people), romantic or otherwise.

3 year. A year in which you will not feel like working very hard. A more frivolous year, good for social activities, and generally having an enjoyable time. Good for creativity, though motivation will be lacking. The perfect year in which to do nothing but enjoy yourself, if possible.

4 year. The year in which you pay for the laziness of the previous one! This year you will want to work hard, and will achieve good results if you have something specific in mind. Unfortunately, most people tend to get bogged down in this year, feeling limited and held down, so many people change jobs in a 4 year. However, it is the worst year to change jobs in as it is the year, rather than the job, that is getting them down, so they jump straight from the frying pan into the fire.

5 year. A year of change and variety, so is the perfect year for changing jobs - or anything else. A good year for travel, taking up new interests, making new friends - generally expecting the unexpected. If you are not doing exciting and different things this year, you will feel slightly unsettled and not know why.

6 year. A year of home and family. So, a good year to get married in, or divorced - as the year can reflect both the positive and negative aspects of the numbers. A good year

for having a baby, or for buying or selling a house, or for doing up an existing house. Most of your energies will be focused on family matters, so you may not always be doing exactly what you want to do because of the needs of people close to you.

7 year. A quieter year, and one in which you will need time on your own to meditate and think about things. An excellent year for learning, either formal education or learning through reading. A year in which many people find God, as the philosophical nature of the 7 comes through strongly at this time.

8 year. A money year. This can be good or bad. It is a good year for buying or selling anything, as financial matters will go your way. However, if you owe everyone money, this is the year in which they try and collect! Many people overdo things in an 8 year, so make sure you have time off during the year for a holiday.

9 year. The completion year of the cycle. A good year for finishing things off and for looking ahead. Better for planning than for doing, as this is a year of endings rather than beginnings. Anything begun in a 9 year tends to end in the 9 year. So, if you get any good ideas in a 9 year try and save them for the 1 year coming up. A 9 year is usually quite an enjoyable year, though you will be asked to let go of things that have outworn their use, so it may have melancholy moments.

We know that Charles is in an 8 year, so if he came to you for a reading you would be able to tell him to be alert for opportunities to make money, but to make sure that he doesn't overdo things.

This is just a little taste of Numerology to try and whet

your appetite. Even if you decide it is not your thing, learn what we have covered here as it is useful information for you to add to your readings, and will also help you understand the motivations and desires of the people you meet.

## CHAPTER TEN

# THE TAROT

The Tarot Cards hold great fascination for many people, and are currently experiencing a real revival. No one knows how old they are, but the oldest ones in existence were made in 1392 for Charles V1 of France. The most popular deck available today is the Waite Tarot, and this is the one you should start with, even though it is highly likely that you will change to another deck once you have mastered the basics. The reason I recommend the Waite deck is that every card has an illustration on it, and this can help you visualise a meaning whilst you are learning. For instance, the Two of Cups shows a picture of people dancing, and this may make you think of a party or a celebration of some sort. In the Marseilles Tarot deck, for example, the Two of Cups is illustrated by a picture of two cups, giving you nothing to go on whilst you are still learning the basic meanings.

The Tarot deck is made up of 78 cards. 22 of these are called the 'Major Arcana' and the remaining 56 are divided into four suits and are called the 'Minor Arcana'. Our present day playing cards are derived from the four suits of the Minor Arcana.

Once you have a deck of your own lay out the 22 cards of the Major Arcana. These are sometimes known as the 'Trump' cards. They start with number 0 (The Fool) and finish with number 21 (The World). When I first started using Tarot Cards I was greatly helped by a paragraph from a book called "The Tarot" by S. L. MacGregor Mathers which brought all the cards of the Major Arcana into a few sentences. I have not seen this paragraph anywhere else, but as it helped me so much, it is included here:

"The Human Will (1) enlightened by Science (2); and manifested by Action (3); should find its Realisation (4) in deeds of Mercy and Beneficence (5). The Wise Disposition (6) of this will give him Victory (7) through Equilibrium (8) and Prudence (9) over the fluctuations of Fortune (10). Fortitude (11), sanctified by Sacrifice of Self (12), will triumph over Death itself (13), and thus a wise Combination (14) will enable him to defy Fate (15). In each Misfortune (16) he will see the Star of Hope (17) shine through the twilight of Deception (18); and ultimate Happiness (19) will be the Result (20). Folly (0), on the other hand, will bring about an evil Reward (21)."

Each card has a meaning which is explained by means of a key-word in the above paragraph.

The Tarot Cards are full of all sorts of symbolism which makes them impossible to adequately explain in just one chapter. It is a fascinating study, though, and can lead you into learning all about the Jewish Cabala, summarised in the symbolic Tree of Life. Every artist has had their own ideas about the meanings of each individual card in the Tarot deck and, consequently, you will find items drawn from Astrology, Numerology, Christianity, Judaism, Mythology, Gnosticism, the Cabala, and even Jung who used the Tarot cards.

In fact it was Carl Jung who came up with the term 'synchronicity', which goes a long way to explaining how the Tarot works. Synchronicity means that the arrangement of the cards after they have been mixed is the only possible combination at that time, so it is not simply a random selection.

I found the best way to learn the cards was to simply play with them and to meditate on different cards. Don't try to do readings, even in fun, when you first get the cards. Simply familiarise yourself with them and gradually assimilate the meanings that are right for you. Get one good book on the Tarot when you buy the cards and stick with the meanings given there until you know them backwards. Once you know the cards, then is the time to read more books and learn what other authors have to say on the subject.

Here is a quick look at the cards in the Tarot Deck.

0 THE FOOL This shows someone moving ahead not looking where he is going. He represents someone with a decision to make.

1 THE MAGICIAN This card shows a strong man with a wand in an upraised hand. It signifies willpower, knowledge and initiative.

2 THE HIGH PRIESTESS This shows a seated lady holding the Book of Science. She represents intuition, wisdom, change and caution.

3 THE EMPRESS This shows a crowned woman sitting on a throne, holding a sceptre in her hand. She represents fruitfulness, happiness, creativity and good fortune.

4 THE EMPEROR This shows a man leaning against a throne, his legs forming a cross. He represents stability, authority and success.

5 THE HIEROPHANT This shows a man wearing the papal tiara, sitting between two pillars. He indicates mercy, good advice, inspiration and religious ideals.

6 THE LOVERS This shows a couple hand in hand. It signifies love, attraction, and success.

7 THE CHARIOT This card shows a conqueror riding in a chariot. It represents triumph, possibility of travel, and success through good judgment.

8 JUSTICE This card depicts a crowned lady sitting on a throne, holding a sword in her right hand and scales in her left. This symbolises equilibrium and justice. It can also indicate a test or ordeal of some sort, and a period of waiting.

9 THE HERMIT This shows a old man holding the lantern of occult science. It indicates caution, a period away from the limelight, delays and diplomacy.

10 THE WHEEL OF FORTUNE This card shows a seven spoked wheel, representing the wheel of fortune, which could be good or bad. It is usually a sign of good luck, something that helps the person progress.

11 STRENGTH This card shows a woman closing the jaws of a lion. It represents courage, strength and self-discipline.

12 THE HANGED MAN This card shows a man hanging upside down from one foot. It represents sacrifice, a period of submission, perhaps punishment.

13 DEATH This card shows a skeleton holding a scythe. It indicates the ending of something and the start of

THE EMPEROR
PARIS TAROT PACK, CIRCA 1500

THE WORLD
PARIS TAROT PACK, CIRCA 1500

EARLY TAROT CARDS

something new. This is the card that frightens most people, but it generally indicates a transformation, rather than a physical death.

14 TEMPERANCE This depicts an angel pouring liquid from one vessel to another. It is a sign of cooperation, partnership, and an indication to proceed only after investigating a situation thoroughly.

15 THE DEVIL This card depicts a horned and winged devil. It indicates temptation, fate and material matters.

16 THE TOWER This card shows a tower collapsing after a flash of lightning. It indicates a loss, disruption and unforeseen disaster.

17 THE STAR A naked lady is pouring water onto the ground from two vases. This card depicts hope, optimism, unexpected help and insight into the future.

18 THE MOON This card shows a dog and a wolf howling at the Moon. It is an indication of deception and hidden enemies. It is a sign of a crisis ahead.

19 THE SUN This card shows two children playing in the Sun's rays. It is a sign of earthly happiness, of prosperity and good fortune.

20 THE DAY OF JUDGMENT This card depicts an angel in heaven blowing a trumpet. It is a sign of a decision made, and a new start beginning. It indicates renewal.

21 THE WORLD This card shows an almost naked lady surrounded by a flowery wreath. It is a sign of success, completion and reward.

QUEEN OF SWORDS
TAROT PACK, CIRCA 1500

ACE OF DENIERS
TAROT PACK, CIRCA 1500

EARLY TAROT CARDS

The Minor Arcana are divided into four suits, each relating to one of the present day suits of cards.

Wands relate to Diamonds
Cups relate to Hearts
Swords relate to Spades
Pentacles relate to Clubs

The suit of Wands relates to work, enterprise and initiative. The suit of Cups relates to love, feelings and emotions, and pleasure. The Swords relate to the intellect, problems and struggle. The Pentacles relate to money, property, all materialistic matters.

Now I could go through and give you the meanings for these fifty six cards individually, but rather than do that, it would be best if you went through the cards, one suit at a time, looking at the pictures and relating each number to its numerological meaning as described in the previous chapter and then relating that to the area which the suit represents.

For instance, look at the Three of Cups. It shows three people dancing in a circle with their cups raised high. The suit of Cups relates to love and pleasure, and the number three relates to having fun and enjoying life. This card obviously means a time of good luck and happiness.

Now let's look at the Eight of Cups - same suit, but different number. This card shows a man walking away from eight cups in the foreground. Eight is the number of money and hard work, so the man is walking away from frivolity and pleasure in search of something better and more meaningful.

Try the Five of Pentacles. Pentacles relates to material

matters and money, whilst five represents change, variety and fluctuation. The card shows two people dressed in rags walking through the snow. It obviously indicates a change for the worse in financial matters. You must remember though, that five is the number that never grows up, so the situation is only temporary as the person will climb out of their temporary difficult situation.

Here's another one - the Ace of Wands. The Ace (number 1) relates to initiative, new starts and enthusiasm, and the suit of Wands relates to work and business. Obviously this card is an indication of a new venture about to begin. The card shows a hand emerging from a cloud holding on to a staff (or wand). In the distance is a castle on top of a hill, showing the rewards of this new beginning.

This covers the numbers One (Ace) to Nine. Number Ten is really number One all over again, but represents the conclusion, rather than the beginning. So the Ace means a start, and the Ten means the conclusion.

The Court cards are just as easy. There are four in the Tarot deck - Pages, Knights (relating to the Jacks in our modern playing cards), Queens and Kings. Pages relate to young people and children. Knights relate to teenagers and young adults. Queens relate to wives, mothers and female friends, whilst Kings relate to fathers, husbands, male friends and givers of advice.

Again we simply relate these to the suits. A Page of Pentacles would indicate a young person who is shrewd and thrifty with money matters. The card shows a young man in the countryside holding a pentacle in his hands.

It might take a little while to get the knack, but once you have it mastered, you will know the meaning of any card you find in a spread instantly.

Take your time in learning the meanings of the cards. If you sit down and work them out parrot-fashion you will forget them all very quickly. It is far better to simply play with the cards and, using keywords, gradually build up your own definitions.

Once you know the cards, you can start on doing 'spreads', which is the name used for laying out the cards. There are many ways of doing these.

If you are familiar with Astrology and know the meanings of the twelve houses, you can simply lay out twelve cards in a circle. Each card relates to the house it is placed in.

If you know little about Astrology, it is better to start with a simple three card spread. Mix the cards up, thinking of a specific question as you do so, and deal three cards in a row face down. The first card relates to the past, the middle card the present and the last card the future. Turn over the first card and interpret it in light of what you knew happened in the past. Then turn over the second card and do the same, relating it to the present. Finally, turn over the last card, which represents the outcome of your question.

This is the simplest spread of all, and you will find it very useful when you have questions you want answered. You will also find it handy when your clients have a question. Some Tarot Card readers do not like other people mixing their cards, so mix them themselves and simply ask their client to lay their hands on the deck after it has been mixed. I prefer to have the client involved, so have the client first mix, then cut the cards, before dealing them out. It is simply a matter of personal preference. Try both and settle on whichever method works best for you.

The most common spread is one called "The Celtic Cross", which is a method using ten cards. The first card laid down represents the person, so you choose this based on the age and sex of your client. This is placed down before the cards are mixed. The second card goes on top of this first card and indicates the present situation. The third card is placed above the first two and represents the clients hopes. The fourth card is placed below the first two and represents basis of the question. The fifth card is placed to the right of the first two and represents the client's past. The sixth card goes to the left of the first two and represents the future. That completes the cross, and the remaining four cards are dealt in a row to the right of the cross. The seventh card represents the client's personality and feelings. The eighth indicates his environment and position in life, the ninth reveal his hopes and fears in the matter, and the tenth and final card shows the final outcome.

It may sound complicated at first, but try it with the cards in your hand and you will find it straightforward. This particular spread was popularised by Arthur Edward Waite, the man behind the Waite Tarot deck. The deck was actually drawn by Pamela Colman Smith, under his direction.

Another spread I find useful is the "Gypsy Spread". Have your sitter (client) mix the cards then cut the pack into two approximately even piles which are placed side by side. Each of these two halves is then cut again, the left hand half being placed above the first two, and the right hand half being placed below. This creates a cross. The top card of the left hand pile represents the past, the top card of the pile at the top of the upright of the cross represents the energies floating around at the present time, the top card of the bottom pile represents the present situation, and the top card of the right hand pile represents the future. This gives a good quick reading if you are wanting something with more information than the three card spread, but less than the Celtic Cross spread.

Whether or not you decide Tarot Cards are right for you, I'm sure you will find them fascinating to experiment with. Use your intuition with the cards and you will amaze yourself with what you accomplish. They make excellent tools for meditation as well. I collect Tarot decks, so often bring out the same card from several different decks and meditate on how each artist has pictured the same card.

It is important that you look after your cards. Naturally, you will wear them out in time - very quickly if you take up Tarot card reading as a profession - so don't regard them as being irreplaceable. Keep them wrapped in a square of silk or velvet (preferably crimson, purple or black in colour) and treat them with care and respect. I like to keep my silk-wrapped cards in a wooden box, as wood comes from a living tree allowing the vibrations of the Universe to reach through to the cards. More of this in the next chapter!

# CHAPTER ELEVEN

# RUNE STONES

Rune stones have regained popularity in recent years. A number of good books have appeared on the subject and it is also possible to buy sets of rune stones at any psychic bookshop.

The stones can be made out of virtually anything - plastic, Fimo, wood, small round pebbles, etc. I have even seen a set painted on seashells. A set consists of twenty five stones each bearing a simple design. Every design has a meaning, and the idea is that once the stones have been mixed in a bag, a handful are removed and tossed (or 'cast') on to a table and the resulting arrangement is read. Only the stones that land face up are read. For simple problems, you can mix the runes and remove just one stone which will answer your question.

If you are going to use rune stones it is important to have a set that means something to you. My first stones were a set I bought made out of some molded composition. They were hard and cold to the touch and I never felt comfortable using them. My next set was made out of balsa wood, and these felt much more comfortable, but were too soft and light to be of much practical use. I then collected some smooth, round river stones and painted the designs on them. I was very happy with this particular set, until a friend offered to make me a set from a branch of a plum tree. These wooden runes, made from a living wood, seem almost magical in power compared to my previous sets, so I heartily recommend that you at least try a set of wooden runes. I also think you should experiment in making your own runes, as this is a good way of learning about them, and also creates an extremely personal set of stones.

The runes have traditional interpretations dating back to the Vikings, as well as modern meanings. Here you will find the modern books on the subject differ, so it will make things easier for you if you study one book thoroughly before reading others. Once you are familiar with what one writer has to say on the subject, you will be in a good position to evaluate what other people have to say, and gradually you will build up your own meanings for each stone.

As you get involved with runes your curiosity will have you searching for the origin of these fascinating symbols. The very word *rune* can be traced back to the Old German *runa*, the Anglo-Saxon *run*, and early Icelandic *runar*.

These words all derive from the Indo-European root word *ru*, which means 'secret'. So the runes have always been a secret language known only to initiates. If you become a rune master you will be part of an extremely old secret tradition. Many theories have been put forward to try and explain the origins of the symbols. As they are all very angular in design it is generally believed that they were carved in stone, which would have made curves difficult to produce.

Here are the basic meanings of each rune. Remember though, that the meanings vary depending on each rune's relationship in a spread with the others, and also if the design on the rune is facing towards you or away from you.

Rune 1. Communication. This rune stands for the Self and mankind in general. It deals with the sitter's contacts with the outside world.

Rune 2. Partnership. This stone indicates that forces outside the sitter's control are working slowly towards a satisfactory outcome. One of the original meanings for this stone was an offering from the Gods, which obviously leads to a satisfactory conclusion.

Rune 3. Signals. This indicates that someone will offer the sitter good advice which should be heeded.

Rune 4. Retreat. The traditional meaning for this is an inheritance, and this meaning still stands, though it could indicate unexpected money rather than an inheritance through a death.

Rune 5. Strength. This is a stone of good fortune, indicating that considerable progress will be made.

Rune 6. Initiation. This is the Rune of Mystery. It could indicate unexpected success, or alternatively, something is revealed that could harm the sitter's reputation.

Rune 7. Restraint. This is a sign that the sitter should exercise caution and proceed slowly and carefully.

Rune 8. Fertility. This relates to Ing, the legendary hero, and indicates news from far away, usually from across water.

Rune 9. Defense. This indicates news from the past, or a solution to a long-standing problem.

Rune 10. Spirit. This indicates new interests, a widening of the sitter's perspective, and safety.

Rune 11. Possessions. An indication of pleasing news, originally cattle and goods from afar.

Rune 12. Joy. A sign of increasing happiness and improvement in the quality of the sitter's life.

Rune 13. Harvest. Good times ahead. A time to relax and enjoy the fruits of one's past efforts.

Rune 14. Links. This governs relationships and is an indication that more attention should be paid in this area.

Rune 15. Warrior. A sign of a love affair that will prosper and grow, despite early indications to the contrary. There may be small problems along the way, but the quality of the relationship is excellent.

Rune 16. Unity. This rune governs home and family, and is a strong indication of marriage if the sitter is unattached.

Rune 17. Changes. This rune is associated with the course of the Sun, and is an indication of travel with a successful outcome.

Rune 18. Flow. This is a sign of a dream or inspiration. Something from the sitter's unconscious will surface and should be acted upon.

Rune 19. Disruption. This is an indication of problems and upheavals, possibly a breakup of a relationship. It can also relate to natural disasters, such as flooding.

Rune 20. Journey. An indication of a trip that will bring happiness.

## THE RUNES AND THEIR MEANINGS

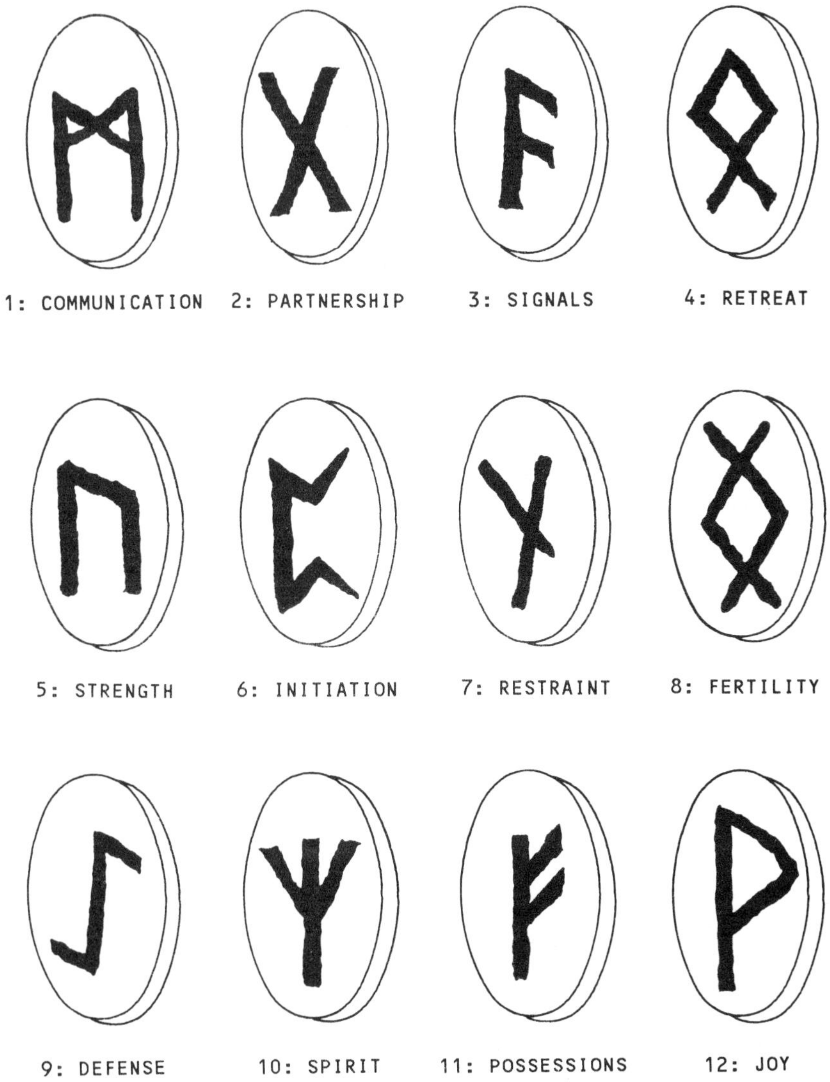

Rune 21. Benefits. An indication of good fortune, luck, a change for the better.

Rune 22. Ambition. A sign that the sitter must set goals and work towards them. Ultimate success through hard work.

Rune 23. Indifference. A half-hearted approach. A loss of interest. This stone relates to ice and freezing conditions.

Rune 24. Sun. An indication that the sitter will be called upon to appraise something carefully, to make a decision. The spotlight (the Sun) will be put upon some aspect of the sitter's life.

Rune 25. Destiny. This stone relates to karma, Kismet, the unknowable. It has to be read with the stones around it. If doing a quick reading for oneself where one stone is taken from the bag, this means that the outcome is out of one's hands - what will be will be.

You may have noticed that most of these meanings are positive. However, when they are reversed, or upside down from your perspective, the opposite of the above meanings apply.

As usual, when first beginning with Runes, ignore your readings until you are completely familiar with them and know the basic meanings by heart. Remember that in the old days novices were forbidden to use their runes for readings for many months after starting their studies.

You may decide not to use Numerology, the Tarot or Rune Stones. Your interests may lie in tea leaf reading, the I Ching - or anything else. However, these last few chapters will not be wasted as you will find that all the occult

## THE RUNES AND THEIR MEANINGS

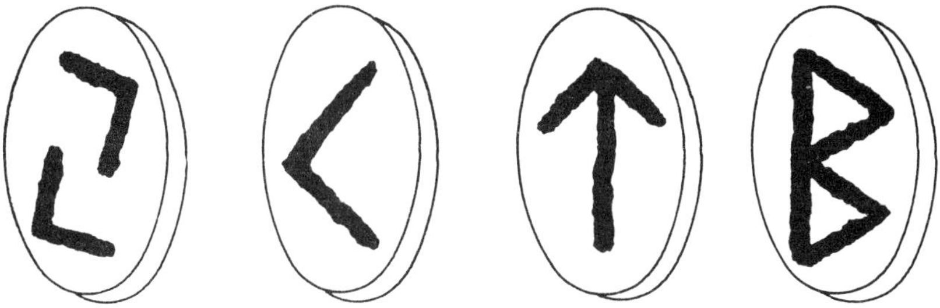

13: HARVEST 14: LINKS 15: WARRIOR 16: UNITY

17: CHANGES 18: FLOW 19: DISRUPTION 20: JOURNEY

21: BENEFITS 22: AMBITION 23: INDIFFERENCE 24: SUN 25: DESTINY

sciences are inter-related, and what you learn from one area can be extremely useful in another, apparently unrelated, subject.

Now let's move on to building up a psychic practice.

CHAPTER TWELVE

# STARTING IN BUSINESS

By the time you have got this far you are bound to have done some readings for friends and members of your family, so your psychic business will have already begun. Word of mouth may have brought in a few more readings, and long term this will be the best form of advertising you can get. People who are happy with their readings will talk about them to others, and this will bring in an increasing amount of business over the years.

However, you are wanting work right now! Before we get on to that, you will have to decide where you are going to have your business. If you are going to run it from home, you will need a special room to see your clients. Nothing is worse than being escorted into a kitchen with dirty dishes everywhere, and being given a reading on the kitchen table with sundry people coming in and out of the room all the time. This may sound a little far-fetched, but I have been given readings in that sort of situation many times. It is certainly not conducive to building up any sort of business.

Ideally, you should have a separate room for your business. Keep it clean and tidy, and decorate it tastefully. Astrological posters can give atmosphere, but keep away from burning incense as some people are allergic to this. There are tax advantages in using a room specifically for business, also. If you can not have a room just for your business, ensure that the room you do use is private and that you won't be interrupted by family and friends whilst you are seeing clients.

The other alternative is to rent an office somewhere. There are advantages and disadvantages to this. The advantages are that you are unlikely to be disturbed whilst giving readings; you may have a business phone there, so that people will contact you there during working hours, rather than at all hours of the day and night at your home; and you can site yourself in a busy area where people can read your sign and come in off the street. However, at the beginning, you may not be able to afford the rent for an office whilst your income is uncertain, so I would recommend that you start at home.

In my own case, I have worked both at home and in an office situation. I prefer an outside office as I like to keep my private life separate from my business, but it can be very frustrating sitting in an office waiting for someone who doesn't turn up for an appointment. I have largely solved this problem now, as I work from a completely separate office under my home. Clients do not have to walk through the house as I have a separate entrance, and if someone fails to turn up I have plenty of things to do at home anyway. I still have the disadvantage of people ringing up for appointments at all hours, but an answerphone partly takes care of that.

So, you have an office or a place to work. How to get business? A business card is essential. Make sure you go to a reputable printer and choose a dignified style for your card. It is better not to claim you can do everything on your card as people will tend not to believe it. A card saying simply "Jean Evans, Clairvoyant" has much more credibility than one saying "Jean Evans, Palmist, Medium,

Clairvoyant, Astrologer, Spiritual Healer, International Psychic and lecturer". People just won't accept that Jean Evans can do all of those things (even if she can), particularly if she is working from her kitchen in the poorest part of town. Make your card as plain and dignified as possible.

Get a large supply of your cards and hand them out to everyone who has a reading. If they are happy with the reading give them half a dozen cards to hand out to their friends. This is a good form of advertising, as often people talk about their readings afterwards but can not remember the name of the person who gave it to them. This way they can give your card to a prospective client. People tend to keep business cards, so this extremely inexpensive form of advertising is a must if you want to develop your business. Have your cards with you everywhere you go, and you will surprise yourself with the number you can hand out. You may be able to leave a small pile at the cash counter of local beauty salons, or pin one up on community notice boards.

In the past I have tried leaflets, four page brochures and even cards printed in full colour, but none of them performed any better than the lowly, inexpensive, single colour business card.

If you are just starting out and have no contacts whatsoever, you may want to place a few advertisements in local newspapers. You will get a lot of phone calls from these advertisements, but very few clients. Also, a large percentage of these will fail to turn up for their appointments. However, the few clients you gain from these advertisements will pass your cards around later, so advertising is definitely well worth the effort and modest expense. I have found no difference in results between large advertisements and small ones, so keep them as small and inexpensive as possible. People who are looking for a psychic reader will find a small advertisement just as easily as a large one. Once you are established you will not need to advertise in local papers as you will obtain more than enough work through referrals. In fact, the main problem with advertising is that most of the people who do it are not very good, so have to advertise to get work as they get no referrals or repeat business. That is why I am not terribly keen on this form of paid advertising. However, if you have no contacts try it as it will bring in some work and get you started.

In setting up a psychic practice you mustn't be modest. Tell everyone what you are doing. You must become a local identity, so that if someone wants a reading you are the person they immediately think about. You may not like to become well known in your locality, but there is no avoiding it. You will build up a reputation in time, anyway, and you must foster this as much as you can as it all pays off in financial terms.

The very best way to build up a psychic practice is to give talks to local groups on your speciality. Work out a twenty or thirty minute talk on your subject and then offer it to as many organisations as you can. I send out a letter telling the secretary about me, about my subject, and how entertaining it will be for their members. Most groups are searching all the time for guest speakers and any psychic topic is sure to attract a good turnout of members.

I give these talks free of charge. Before my talk I give everyone a printed sheet of information on whatever the subject is, and naturally enough, this includes my name and phone number. You will find people keep these giveaways and you can get work from them years after you handed them out. After my talk I ask for any questions, and always someone will ask if I do private readings. This gives me the perfect opportunity to tell everyone what I do, how long the readings take and how much I charge. I do not recall ever giving a talk where this question was not asked, but if it ever occurred I would simply finish up by saying that I am available for private readings and my phone number is on the printed sheet.

Another excellent way of building your business up quickly is to give brief readings in a fleamarket or psychic fair. In these situations I have a pile of business cards in front of me and these are taken by people who could intend to contact me privately. I give everyone who has a quick reading the same giveaway I use at my talks, and also explain to them that this is just a quick reading and I can go into much more detail if they come and see me privately. After a few weeks in a fleamarket situation your business should be well established.

You should make contact with the other psychic readers in your area. I know they are your opposition, but you can also work in with them. If you recommend Joe Bloggs to one of your clients as he is particularly good at something you don't do, he is likely to recommend one of his clients to you. This is beneficial to you both and can lead to a lot of increased work.

You should also become involved in whatever psychic groups or development circles there may be in your neighbourhood. This serves two purposes: you become known to a wider circle of people as being involved in the psychic world, and you gain access to a large group of potential clients.

I also do a few 'barter' readings. For instance, a month ago I did a reading for a lady who owns a fashion shop. Instead of receiving payment, my wife was able to select a cardigan for herself. No money changed hands, but we were both happy! This can be a good source of extra readings. I used to be a bit reluctant to broach the subject, but now often suggest a swap.

Another way to build up your business is to offer to go to people's homes and do the readings there. I insist on a minimum of three people to make the journey worth my while. I know some readers who do all of their work in other people's homes, and this could appeal to you too, but I prefer to work in my own surroundings.

If there is a psychic bookshop near you, they may be happy for you to give readings on the premises. I used to do this at one stage and gave the shop ten per cent of my earnings. The shop used to make the bookings for me and I'd go in one day a week and do the readings. Even if the shop is not keen on having you give readings there, they will generally allow you to put up a small advertisement for your services. This will bring in some work, but you will be competing with a large array of other psychics. Make sure that your advertisement is of better quality than the others to attract attention.

When you are starting out you will probably be charging a little bit less than your competition. As your experience increases you should charge more for your time and effort. It is impossible to quote figures here as so much depends on where you live. I live in a city of a million people and am charging a price that would be totally unacceptable in a town of thirty thousand. The best way is to find out what everyone else is charging and then charge about the same - or a little bit more. Being the cheapest does not always work. If you charge ten per cent more than someone else, you are seen by the public as being better. If you charge less, you are seen as not being as good! So do not underprice your services. Ask a friend to contact the other readers in your locality to find out what they are charging, as they may not give you their correct fees if you ask them direct. Right from the start ensure that your readings are worth more than your competitors' readings. Give value for money and you will never lack for work.

## CHAPTER THIRTEEN

# BUILDING UP YOUR BUSINESS

You will find it comparatively easy to build up your business. All you have to do is give good readings and your fame will gradually spread. However, I have found it useful to do a few extra things to increase business in the quiet periods. Where I live all the psychics are quiet from the beginning of December until the end of February. This is a quarter of a year! Where you live the pattern may be different, but you can be certain that some times will be quieter than others. For instance, in school holidays I am seldom busy because any extra money is spent on the children rather than in having a reading. So I have developed a system of getting extra work in these quiet periods.

Firstly, I keep a record of everyone who comes to see me. This includes their name, address and date of birth. I can do a number of things with this information. Twelve months after their consultation with me I send them a little note reminding them of this and suggesting they return for an update. A large percentage do.

With the date of birth I can send them a birthday card. I know of no other psychic who does this, but it is a fantastic way of building up goodwill. You become regarded as a friend by your client. They forget that they have given me all this information in the course of the reading, so are amazed that I remember their birthday! This encourages repeat business, and keeps your name in the client's mind. Many, many times my card has been the only card the client received on their birthday, so it is more than appreciated - it is treasured!

I also produce a little newsletter called "Psychic Update". This is a four page, A4 sized, newsletter. It contains articles about psychic research, how to work out your lucky number, an astrological guide, and other similar articles. These articles come from my own reading and research and are very easy to compile as they are all written at a simple, 'pop' level. Along with the articles I include a few advertisements for my own services, suggesting it is time they came and saw me again. This newsletter appears whenever business gets quiet and I send it to all the people on my mailing list who I haven't seen for at least twelve months. It is a simply fantastic way of gaining business in the quiet periods. People are delighted to get a free newsletter. They keep it as it contains useful information, it makes them think of me, and many of them ring and make a booking. During the quiet periods all the other psychics ring each other to complain about how quiet it is. They can't believe how I always seem to be busy! They know about my newsletter, but none of them can be bothered to sit down and write one. Even if they did, none of them keep mailing lists, so would have no one to send it to. I can write, produce and post a "Psychic Update" in less than two days, and that two days work can keep me busy throughout three normally quiet months. I also leave copies of the "Psychic Update" in public libraries, and these are picked up by people who could become clients.

The other way of building up your business also involves writing. I know this does not appeal to everyone, but it can pay enormous dividends in financial terms. All you do is become the local authority in anything to do with the psychic. You do this by writing articles for magazines and newspapers. The large circulation, national magazines may not publish your work, but your local, free newspapers will be delighted to print them as they are always looking for material to disguise the fact that they are basically enormous advertisements! They probably will not pay you for these articles, but you will gain a steady stream of new clients who will be impressed that you are not only a psychic, but an author as well!

You should also look for opportunities to write letters to the paper. These situations occur more frequently than you may think. In the last few weeks the papers have been full of reports of UFO's, so I sat down a wrote a letter giving my views on the subject. It was duly published with my name underneath, and sure enough my phone was busy the day it appeared!

The big advantage of anything appearing in print, either by or about you, is that you can use it forever. Put a number of articles together, and get your quick printer to run off a thousand. You can give these away to clients and hand them out at your talks. These will increase your prestige and reputation enormously - not to mention your bank account.

Talkback programmes are very popular on the radio and you should try and get on to one of these. Don't wait to be invited. Ring the announcer shortly after he gets off air, tell him briefly about yourself and your areas of expertise and offer to send in a bunch of clippings and information about you. He may not be interested in the psychic, but he is concerned about ratings and will be aware of the public interest in the subject, so will be delighted to see what you send him. A few days after posting the information ring him again, and you are bound to receive an invitation to appear on the programme. If he is not interested, simply try someone else. Appearing on the radio (or television) is a fantastic free advertisement for you and will bring in a lot of work, often more than you can handle.

In time you will probably find it worthwhile investing in a computer to help you keep your mailing lists. My computer can tell me instantly what clients came to see me twelve months ago (or any other period I care to specify), and then it can print out labels so I can do a mailing to these people automatically. I can go on and do something else whilst it is doing this. The computer can also tell me which of my clients is having a birthday in the next week, how many times any specific client has been to see me, and all sorts of other information. I have several thousand names in my computer now, so it is an essential part of my business. I don't recommend that you invest in one in the early stages though. I used to keep my clients names and addresses in a shoe box and this worked well until I outgrew the box.

## CHAPTER FOURTEEN

# CONCLUSION

I have thoroughly enjoyed writing this book, and hope that you have not only enjoyed it, but are using it to build up your own psychic practice. I doubt that there is any other business that can be built up so quickly and so cheaply and that can help your clients improve their lives whilst making you a considerable income! Once you have developed your psychic abilities to the stage that you can give satisfactory, helpful readings you will become a valuable part of the community. It is important though, that you keep on learning and developing your abilities, so that your readings will become better and better as you progress in this fascinating field.

Don't forget the exercises in the earlier chapters, either, as they can be useful in helping you relax after a day of helping others. I find giving readings is somehow stimulating and draining at the same time. So ensure that you do give yourself time off. For one whole year I saw eight people every day and was out either talking or giving readings virtually every night. It did wonders for my bank balance, but took its toll in terms of my health, and I was also aware that my readings were not as good as they should have been. So allow time for rest, and make sure you take regular holidays. Actually, once you have been in business for a while, you will discover that you can take wonderful overseas holidays free of charge, as you can do a few readings each day in your hotel room! I doubt if there is any business as easily transportable as this one.

Make sure that you are honest with your clients. It is much better long term to tell a client that you don't know the answer, rather than attempt an answer which could be misleading and totally wrong. In the early stages you may find it hard to admit that you do not know the answer to a question, but you will sleep more easily at night and build your business on a sounder foundation if you are completely honest with your clients. I believe that we can see a lot of things, but some things are not meant to be known.

You won't master everything in this book overnight, but with a little bit of effort every day you will amaze yourself at how quickly your abilities grow.

I'm looking forward to the day when I can come to you for a reading!